OU

OUT OF BOUNDS

The story of Malcolm Worsley
Prisoner to Probation Officer

Judith Wigley

Highland Books

ISBN NO: 0 946616 88 4

Copyright © Judith Wigley 1992

British Library Cataloguing-in-Publication Data. A
catalogue record for this book is available from the
British Library

Published by Highland Books, an imprint of Inter
Publishing Service (IPS) Ltd, Williams Building,
Woodbridge Meadows, Guildford, Surrey GUI 1BH

Printed in the UK by HarperCollins Manufacturing,
Glasgow.

Cover photograph by Mark Keefe.

Contents

Acknowledgements

I am deeply grateful to Malcolm for giving me the opportunity to write this very special story. It was my privilege. But my gratitude extends to the whole Worsley family—Jennifer, Helen and Paul—for allowing me to share in their lives both individually and corporately as a family. Their openness, honesty and patience throughout the period of research and writing will not be forgotten. Neither will the friendship, fellowship and fun that we've had together as families.

My special thanks go to the many people, too many to name, who took time to recall their memories and experiences of working with Malcolm; in particular, the ex-members of the Lindley Lodge Community in Nuneaton.

My thanks to Sue Rosseter and Jim Heaton for their reading of the manuscript and correction of numerous spelling errors! I remain indebted to my special friends who have been constant in prayer throughout and who I know would not wish to be named.

Acknowledgements

Last but not least, I thank my children for allowing me to work through the early mornings of their 1991 summer holiday!

Judith Wigley

Foreword

Just occasionally you meet a person whose story, when it is told to you, is so gripping and remarkable that you know, even as you listen to it pouring out, that it is going to remain a living part of your own heart and mind permanently.

Malcolm Worsley is one of that rare band of people whose account of his life has had that kind of effect on me. When he came into my study in Coventry and we got talking and I invited him to tell me something of the experience which is the subject of this book, I was completely gripped by it. It wasn't until we had been talking for some time that I realised that I was, in fact, the second Bishop of Coventry to receive a blessing from this man.

The first was my great predecessor, Bishop Cuthbert Bardsley, who, when Malcolm came to see him in this same study and told him something of the same testimony, actually physically gave him his blessing. Whereupon, Malcolm spontaneously returned the compliment, as you will read in the book. No wonder Bishop Cuthbert was absolutely delighted! For me also it was a joy to hear Malcolm and then pray with him.

I am delighted that now Malcolm's story has been so clearly, vividly and effectively put into writing by the wife of a vicar who played a key part in its unfolding. I am certain it will have the same vital effect on all those who read it that it has had on me.

This is essentially a description of how a person can be remade by the grace of God. We often hear and talk about Jesus Christ having the power to change people's lives, 'If anyone be in Christ he is a new creation, a new being' (2 Corinthians 5:17). Many of us know, at least to some extent, that this has been true in our own lives. But it does something amazing for our faith and for our whole hope and expectation of what God can bring about in ourselves and in others when we read a book like this, the record of someone whose whole character and nature has been so obviously and totally renewed and redeemed. The first sentences of this book and the last come together, and we find Malcolm re-entering the same prison he first arrived at as an inmate, now to be a member of its staff. Between those two entries lies a quite extraordinary change. A whole new world has truly come into existence.

As we enter into the story, in the way in which its author, Judith Wigley, and its subject, Malcolm Worsley, have enabled us to do, we will find that we ourselves are profoundly affected by it. Do we really *want* God to help us to change? Do we really *believe* God can help us? Could the same miracle occur in our own lives as so manifestly comes to pass in the life of this seemingly helpless and hopeless figure, as he is

when we first meet him in these chapters? It
is the account of a miracle of healing and of
transformation taking steady, convincing effect.

The grace of God which grasps and transforms
Malcolm comes to him through the word of God,
the Bible which Max Wigley first puts into his
hand. It comes to him in the solitude of his
cell, meeting him in his inmost being on his
own. It is profoundly moving to read of his
astonishing ministry to his fellow prisoners,
some of whom became disciples with him. God's
grace also comes to him through the community
and people of Christ. It comes first through the
Vicar himself, Max Wigley, through Will Barker,
his prison visitor, through Lindley Lodge and the
team and community there, through St James,
Weddington, and Guy and Helen Cornwall-Jones;
and so through many in Nuneaton and in the
Diocese of Coventry. Above all it comes to him
through that remarkable helpmeet and part-
ner, Jennifer, who truly suffers and grows with
Malcolm as he comes into the fullness of his ministry to the homeless, the drop-outs, the victims
of society, so needy then as now—and eventually
to youngsters on probation and prisoners.

There are so many points at which this grace
restores and renews and heals not only Malcolm,
but those to whom he is sent, even those whom
earlier in his life he had injured. There is more to
touch us and to convict us and to move us on every
page as we go on to the end of this part of the
story. And I can assure you that when you meet
Malcolm now, the power of that grace reaches out
through him to touch you afresh. I believe and

hope that this tale will have a freshly converting influence upon whoever picks it up and begins to read. I am certain it will be a blessing to many, bishops included! I dare to pray that it will help significantly in bringing about the fundamental change in our own hearts and lives, and in the life of our church and society, which we desperately need today.

+Simon Coventry

One

Out of Bounds

Malcolm stood facing the door. On it was a sign which read OUT OF BOUNDS. Without hesitating he turned and walked back down along the corridor he had just left. It was the first day of his new job at Haverigg Prison, and he felt sure that this was the route to his new office. 'Obviously not,' he told to himself, 'there must be another way that I don't know of.' No sooner had the thought crossed his mind than he realised what he had done.

Ten paces from the door with his back to the sign he stood absolutely still, hardly daring to breathe. His body felt paralysed. Somewhere in the distance a voice was shouting, 'Malcolm, Malcolm, you have just walked away from a sign intended for a prisoner.' It was loud and repetitive, but it was some time before the words made any sense. When they did, a terrifying uncertainty came over him. *Who was he and what was he doing in this place*? Confused and bewildered he realised that this was turning into one of the most traumatic moments of his life.

'Stop it, pull yourself together, why now, why

now?' he said over and over again, in an attempt to regain control of his now trembling body. After all it wasn't the first time he had returned to Haverigg since that unforgettable departure nearly twenty years earlier. His last post, based in Whitehaven with Cumbria Probation Services, had brought him here on many occasions to visit clients who were serving sentences inside Haverigg. Some of those visits had been recent. But today was definitely different.

His appointment as probation officer to Haverigg Prison had changed things considerably and the fact that he was here to stay hit him hard. It wasn't a fleeting visit of an hour or two that he could brace himself for, knowing full well that he'd be able to walk away until the next time, perhaps weeks or even months later. Today was the beginning of a much longer sentence. Every morning he would walk through the gates, past security and into the administration department. Every day he would face what had, a long time ago, been his nightmare. There was no running away from the past. Right now he knew he was reliving the nightmare, and it was hurting. Somebody had opened the floodgates, and Malcolm was drowning in a swamp of painful memories. Yes, he had been a convicted criminal and Haverigg had been his prison.

It wasn't the sight of the building that had gripped him; he was familiar enough with that. No, it was the sudden reminder of what life here had been like and the effect it had had on him as a person. Even though twenty years had passed since his last sentence, it was the

old Malcolm who confronted him now. What
little dignity and self-worth he'd managed to
salvage through the early years of life had been
well and truly squashed in places of this kind.
A prison sentence was the removal of rights,
the restraint of all freedom. But for Malcolm
it had been much more than that. Years of
being locked up had suppressed parts of him
to the point of destruction. He remembered it
all too clearly.

Haverigg was category C, a semi-open prison.
There were no small cells, heavy doors and great
bundles of keys as in Armley, Risley, Liverpool,
Wormwood Scrubs and so many of the others
he had experienced. The dormitories, recreation
facilities and industrial work rooms were meant
to create a less restrained environment, but the
result for him was quite the reverse. Every
waking moment was controlled and regimented
by the presence of prison officers. Locked in a
cell, you could at least kid yourself that you
were locking the system out and retain some
degree of privacy for part of the day. But here
you were under observation twenty-four hours a
day living in fear of being 'nicked' for walking
too fast, having a shoe lace untied, breathing too
heavily, or having the wrong expression on your
face. Or at least, at times, it felt that way. The
consequences of such 'sins' were severe and to
be avoided at all costs. Allowances and rations
could be forfeited, extra work duties enforced;
but the ultimate in the old days was three days
in the 'chokey block' in solitary with just bread
and water to keep you alive. Each time you went

down, a part of you never returned; it was a long drawn out execution.

Once 'inside' you became a number, a nobody. You ate, slept, worked and exercised when told to. Even the timing of going to the loo was dictated by prison officers. There was no space for personality or individuality. The memories were deeply engrained in Malcolm, and some experiences still hurt when he recalled them. Not even twenty years of rebuilding and restoring his life had fully removed the deep psychological damage of these prison years. Some memories, like the incident at Wormwood, haunt him to this day.

It was a new sentence. As usual he was petrified, but more so this time because it was Wormwood—and London. He had heard many tales about the prison and its inmates, none of which had given cause for encouragement. Big-time criminals, hardened prison officers and the vastness of the whole institution made him feel physically sick. With no letters to receive, no one to write to and certainly no hope of visitors, he didn't know if he'd survive the sentence.

Prison wages weren't issued in those days: just tobacco and match allowances when the work was completed. They became the lifeline of many new convicts like Malcolm whose nerves were well and truly frayed. As usual his first task was to scrub the cell floor. In desperation for the small quantity of tobacco that would make up two, perhaps three, cigarettes he slaved away until the grain in the wooden floor stood out. It was worth every ounce of energy for the release that the tobacco would bring to his shattered nerves.

Allowances were issued after the mid-day meal
and so it was with great eagerness that Malcolm
returned to his cell that lunchtime. The sight
that faced him still troubles him to this day.
Written in thick black wax (used by prisoners
for waxing the thread on post office sacks) and
sprawled across the cell floor in large, bold capital
letters were the words **'THIS IS FILTHY'**. There
was no tobacco, no matches—just a bucket and
scrubbing brush and the instructions to do it
again. It was a kick in the face, stomach and
groin—all in one blow. It was a violent assault
upon the spirit of a helpless man who now lay
distraught in a quivering, blubbering heap on the
cell floor. A prison officer looked on, revelling in
the sight. His mission had been accomplished.

That day in Wormwood felt like yesterday, not
twenty or thirty years ago. How could he walk
through the door, past the sign that had so suddenly removed the last twenty years from his life?
The pain, the struggle, the stigma should have
been behind him, yet here he was, responding
as an inmate. He wanted to pinch himself in
the hope that he'd wake up from what had been
just a bad dream; but, no, this was a living
nightmare. There had been other crises over the
years, hurdles to jump or knock down but none
as devastating as this moment. Malcolm's two
lives, past and present, had collided in the most
extraordinary way.

He wasn't sure if he had the energy to fight,
something that he had grown accustomed to
doing. The most he could manage was a cry
from the heart, 'O God, help!' He stood for what

seemed an eternity wondering if he would ever move again. Gradually a calm came over him and the words of the prison officer who released him from Haverigg at the end of his seventh and final sentence came into his mind: 'You'll be back, Worsley, I know your type. You'll be back.' 'Yes', he said quietly to himself, 'I *am* back. He was right.' It wasn't in the manner expected, but Malcolm Worsley was back inside Haverigg Prison. Perhaps there had been a purpose in this moment after all.

Twenty years had passed and with them a series of unbelievable events, not least the invitation from the prison governor to take up this very position, bringing him to this point. He had status and authority given to him by the prison service, and he had every right to walk through those doors.

Humbled and yet quietly confident in the God who had turned his life upside down, he lifted his head, turned slowly, and walked back down the corridor, through the door, past the sign, and into his office.

Two

Life on the Run

The journey from Preston to Bradford was a
well-worn route for Malcolm, and he felt sure
he could have driven it blind-folded. Tonight he
needed to do just that. He ached all over from
large, inflamed bruises that spread across his
body; and his face throbbed with the pain of
several breaks in the jaw bone. His shoulder was
badly dislocated.

It was just twenty-four hours since he had discharged himself from hospital. What should have
been at least a week's stay turned out to be only
a day. Within that time doctors had implanted
wire into his face to hold the jaw bone together in
the hope that it might heal. Eating had become a
physical impossibility, and his mouth opened just
far enough to get a drinking straw between his
lips. The slightest movement resulted in excru-
ciating pain. Nursing staff pleaded with him to
stay, knowing there was a high risk of infection
in the wound and explaining just how critical it
was that the wire was removed at the appropriate time and in proper sterile conditions. But
Malcolm refused, collected the few belongings

he had, and walked out. Pushing all thoughts
of infection and further damage to his face out of
his mind, he removed the wire himself, using the
only instrument he could find—a pair of pliers.

He drove the stolen vehicle on into the dark
and bitterly cold night grateful for the detailed
knowledge of every set of lights, crossroads and
road bend he would meet. The only difference
was the car, depending on what had been simplest to 'acquire' on that particular night. His
destination might well have been Bradford, but
the journey itself was aimless. It was one of
many made 'on the run': that repeated process
of moving from place to place in the hope that it
would avoid or at least delay by days, weeks or
sometimes months, the inevitable arrest by the
police. Malcolm always knew he'd be arrested
eventually as he wasn't a good or successful
criminal; it was only a matter of time before
he'd return to the familiar surroundings of one
or other prison to serve yet another sentence.
There, the cycle would start again.

He had never been particularly successful in
anything, though there was no glaring or obvious reason for his failure. He couldn't claim
a deprived or disadvantaged background and
had certainly received as many opportunities
as others of his generation and social background. His hard-working Lancashire parents
were proud of their four children, Malcolm being
the first. Like the others, he was far from stupid;
they had all taken full advantage of openings
that came their way. Bright and intelligent maybe—but Malcolm, like many young men of his

age, was bored. Despite being told on many occasions that he had ability and potential, he failed to use it.

By the time he had left school at 15 he was all too familiar with failure. It dampened what enthusiasm he had and left him with little incentive to achieve anything in life. Reluctantly he agreed to join his father's building firm as an apprentice and over a period of time acquired a skill that gave him something of lasting value. Those five years offered a degree of stability and security, which all came to a sudden end when at 20, along with many of his peers, he was called up for National Service.

Army life brought drastic changes to Malcolm's lifestyle. It was his first real move away from home and threw him into a regimented work routine that was totally foreign. He responded only because he had to and made few attempts to face the implications of war and the consequences it might have for him at this stage of his life. But the horrific realities dawned on him all too soon—when he was sent into action. Having set sail for the Suez Canal, expecting to join other British forces already engaged in heavy fighting, it came as a shock to be redirected to Malaya. During the course of travel the Suez crisis had come to an end and the troop in which Malcolm served was sent to combat communist terrorists under the leadership of Chin Peng in Malaya, in what became known as the Malayan War. Malaya in war time was not a pretty experience. Nothing could prepare them for the shocking conditions in which Malcolm

and other young soldiers were expected to live
and fight. There could be no pretence; it wasn't
a game. The realities of jungle warfare were
beyond the wildest of human imaginations: the
stench, intense heat, leeches, ringworm and horrific jungle sores were just the beginning. Death,
fear, suspicion, terrorism and the sheer hopelessness of many Chinese and Malays faced him
every day. It became too much to bear; there was
no way out.

Malcolm's only relief came in the form of
rum or Anchor and Tiger bitter. Heavy drinking was quite acceptable in the army, almost
expected, and supplies readily available. It dulled
the senses, took away the pain and distanced
the reality of suffering. He welcomed it with
open hands and mouth, oblivious to the ever-
increasing quantities he was drinking and the
serious long-term effects it would have upon his
life. As he had grown accustomed to, he lived only
for the moment.

The only thing he valued about army life was
the fact that he rarely had to think for himself.
He was told when to work, when to sleep, eat
and drink! When his demob came in 1959, he
received it with a mixture of relief and shock.
Yes, he was desperate to leave the horror of
Malaya behind, but demob also meant losing a
whole framework for his life. Suddenly alone and
isolated, his only familiar link with the past three
years was drink. It became a source of comfort
and consolation, serving once again to distance
the present. Meanwhile he had little desire to
face future responsibility in any form.

Yet again circumstances eventually forced Malcolm into action. Josephine, his girlfriend since before the war, announced that she was pregnant. Social and family pressures of the day insisted upon marriage, and everything seemed to happen very quickly. At the age of twenty-three Malcolm found himself a husband and father to a son, named Alan. Stephen, their second child, arrived only eighteen months later.

Like Malaya, family life wasn't something he had consciously and deliberately chosen; rather, it was thrust upon him. Nonetheless, Josephine and his two sons belonged to him; they, along with the drink, became his source of security and comfort. Their home was small and unassuming, a place where he spent very little time, but it was somewhere to belong that was very important to him. He failed miserably as a husband and a father and knew it. When he bothered to work, he was capable of earning good money but equally capable of squandering every penny on drink and gambling. Josephine could never rely on Malcolm earning a regular income, and even on special occasions such as Christmas and the boys' birthdays he failed to show any concern for their well-being or happiness. They regularly went without some of the most basic needs. He could never be trusted and despite promise after promise his every word soon became meaningless to the family.

The urge to drink was greater and stronger than any desire he knew. Every bit of reason deserted him when the longing for alcohol took over. For most of the time drink controlled his life

and dictated to him his every waking moment. So
it was no surprise to friends, family and neighbours when Josephine decided she could take no
more. He had long since deserted her and the
children, only returning home when the money
ran out or there was nowhere else to go. At those
times he was always drunk. Josephine had tried
to help, but for the sake of the children she knew
that she had to get out of the relationship. With
the help and support of her parents who, with
good cause, disliked their son-in-law intensely,
she took the boys away to stay with an aunt,
leaving no forwarding address.

While Malcolm had spent precious little time
at home, the absence of both his wife and children
was sheer torture to him. He had no one and
nothing to call his own. His parents, brothers
and sister had tried many times to bail him out
of his trouble and give support, but each time he
abused their trust and took advantage of their
expressions of care and concern. On numerous
occasions he had tried to assure them that 'this'
time would be different, the last time and never
again . . . until, of course, the next time. Malcolm
had no self-control. How it pained them to watch
their son and brother wreck both his own life and
the lives of others.

Desperation drove Malcolm until he found
his family in Barnsley, Yorkshire. Penniless
as usual, he booked into a small hotel nearby
knowing full well that he couldn't pay the bill.
He wanted a chance to plead with them, to beg
them to take him back, making all the same
promises they had heard many times previously.

Not surprisingly he failed to convince Josephine, but the price of his unpaid hotel bill was costly. It was the first of many prison sentences to come, the beginning of the downward spiral of the next eight years. It was also the seal on his broken marriage. Josephine filed for divorce and finally succeeded in cutting the ties from her enstraged and drunken husband. Malcolm could never remember which sentence he was serving when he signed the divorce papers but he knew Josephine and the boys were unlikely to be part of his life again.

From this time onwards Malcolm's life took on the pattern of ever-decreasing circles. Individual incidents may well have varied, but the overall direction was always the same, round and round, down and down. Prison, release, drink, failure to work, steal in order to eat, months on the run, then finally the inevitable arrest and prison once more. At first Malcolm sincerely believed he could break free and start again. He made several determined efforts with limited success. The pittance of cash and travel warrant given by the Discharged Prisoners Association was barely enough to get him home, never mind provide food and shelter. As for so many released convicts there was never anyone to meet him, and he had no place to go. The routine became a ritual. Find rooms, persuade the landlady to give written evidence of the booking, queue at the the Supplementary Benefit Office for rent money, go to the pub, drink the entire week's allowance and not have anything with which to pay the rent or eat.

Following one particularly painful fifteen-month stretch 'inside', Malcolm decided it would be the last. He planned carefully how it would happen. If he could survive a fifteen-month sentence, he reasoned, surely a self-imposed sentence of one week was easy? Having secured a room for £2 a week he budgeted carefully, bought the bare essentials—a tablet of soap, a razor, some bread and margarine. His T-shirt became his towel, and there were no other food luxuries. On this occasion he found a job on a building site working hard, long hours. Each evening he returned to his 'cell', ate his bread and margarine, forbidding himself to go out, and determined to survive the sentence.

All went well and he collected what he saw as the first of many pay packets, his first real means to survival for some time. The sense of achievement was great and he felt sure that a celebration was called for. But there was only one kind of celebration in Malcolm's books, and he took himself off to the pub to enjoy his ration of just one drink. As he stood at the bar the £15 burned fiercely into his thirst for alcohol. He failed to recognise that he was incapable of having just one drink. Gradually as the evening wore on he drank through his only means of survival, a week's wage.

Once on the alcohol trail again, he'd do anything to satisfy the burning desire. Breaking into gas and electric meters, stealing any available cash, selling the contents of his rented room, acquiring goods on hire purchase in order to sell them for cash, stealing cheque books, credit cards and the like. How he got the money was unimportant as long as he did it. The single goal in life was to quench that insatiable thirst for alcohol, the end of which was always prison.

As time passed he found fewer friends on the outside who were prepared to help and increasing numbers of criminals who wanted his services. Prison was the dustbin of society where one could easily perfect a crime. Malcolm did just that. Word got around as to his usefulness, and each release provided him with increased opportunities for more serious crime. In his desire to be accepted and needed he set about the task of proving himself worthy in the eyes of his criminal peers. The petty crimes became more serious, the company more dangerous, and the prison sentences longer.

* * *

This particular night, driving from Preston to Bradford, was on the surface typical of many in the last eight years. The only difference lay in the fact that Malcolm knew he couldn't go on. Perhaps it was the intense pain on this occasion; the broken jaw, dislocated shoulder and sore bruises all reminded him of the events of the last few days. The 'gang' he had been working with this time had been excessively violent. The more money 'earned', the greedier he became, most of the cash being used to buy alcohol or friendship. But on this last job Malcolm had double-crossed the others. Having stolen large numbers of television sets from a Yorkshire firm, he was to sell them to contacts in Preston and then share out the money. Instead he had kept it all for himself and was now paying bitterly for his failure. Such were 'friends' in the criminal world. Once more he found himself on the run from police, friends and enemies, with nowhere to go.

With the rain beating against the windscreen of the car, it was becoming increasingly difficult to see out or concentrate on driving, so he pulled into a lay-by at the side of the road. It was cold and bleak. Behind him the lights of the Samlesbury Airfield glared into the darkness. Malcolm lowered his head slowly onto the steering wheel, the pain throbbing throughout his entire body. At first the tears fell slowly and silently, but then the floodgates opened. Soon his whole body heaved with the sobbing of a lost and destitute child. He cried out, 'God help me—I'm in a mess.'

It was hardly a prayer as he had no idea to whom or what he might be talking. It was more a desperate cry into the darkness in the hope that someone or something might reply.

Three

A Bradford Vicar

Over a few days, the pain in Malcolm's jaw eased, leaving a dull, aching sensation. His hopelessness also lost some of its intensity or at least didn't surface again in quite the same desperation as on that night. He knew it would always linger inside and unlike his jaw would take more than time to heal. He longed to get out of the vicious circle he was trapped in but had tried many times and failed. Somehow he knew that it wasn't something he could do by himself.

Once in Bradford he flitted from place to place, grabbing every offer of accommodation and food as he went. Even within a city he needed to keep on the move, never staying in any one patch for too long for fear that the news of his whereabouts would reach the wrong ears. Some of the members of the crime syndicate he had worked with lived close to Malcolm's girlfriend's house, on one of the many large council estates in the city. News travelled fast, in these parts especially. Though Margaret's was the obvious place for him to stay, it was far too dangerous to be seen there, so his calls were fleeting and often at night.

During one particular visit he managed to persuade her to let him take her four-year-old son Philip with him for a while. He'd be some company, and Malcolm knew it was always easier to secure sympathy, food and money with a child as people rarely had the heart to turn away a child in need. More importantly the police would be reluctant to stop him with a child sitting in the front seat of a car. He knew all the tricks of the trade and was not beyond even using children to further his selfish ends when it suited him.

Having Philip with him worked well for a time until Malcolm started to feel very uneasy, convinced not only that the police knew he was in town but that he was part of the CID morning briefing. He'd been around for too long, it was time to go—and fast. Normally he would have taken off in whatever vehicle he had in his possession at the time or in one he could acquire quickly, but this time it wasn't quite so easy; Philip was an enormous obstacle. Keeping Philip was no longer practical and might place the child in danger, yet he knew there was far too great a risk involved in returning him to Margaret on the estate, where his pursuers would be waiting for him. There was only one way it could be resolved. In order to ensure Philip's safety he had to find a 'go-between', someone to do the job for him. Rather impulsively, he decided on a vicar.

St John's Church, Great Horton, towered above the surrounding buildings. Built on the hillside, its black Yorkshire stone could be seen for miles around the city. It wasn't the church building itself that Malcolm had noticed especially but the large bill-board positioned on the corner of the side street close by, clearly visible to all who travelled up Great Horton Road from the city centre. Passengers on the top deck of buses had a particularly close encounter with the large bold letters!

Malcolm had driven past regularly, always automatically reading the many and varied messages: JESUS LIVES, CHRIST DIED FOR YOUR SINS, NEW LIFE IN JESUS. But the one that had stayed with him said, JESUS CHRIST CAN CHANGE YOUR LIFE. Occasionally it would be a longer message with some kind of abbreviated word and numbers following it. His vague recollections from Sunday School days told him that those words came from the Bible. Though he had never given much thought to what he read, what struck him more than anything was that the people responsible for putting up the posters obviously felt they had something important to say to others, the passers-by. Those people, he presumed, rightly so, must belong to the church behind. It seemed a good place to start looking for a vicar.

A second smaller notice board outside the church provided Malcolm with the information he needed—the name and address of the vicar. With no time to waste he walked several hundred yards up the road to the vicarage.

Early morning callers were not unusual at the Dracup Road vicarage, especially the needy, homeless and hungry. The recently appointed young vicar was already used to their often exaggerated tales and longed for the wisdom

and discernment to distinguish between those
genuinely in need and others fabricating some
story in the hope of securing sympathy and cash.
It wasn't easy, especially when you discover
that your vicarage has become one of the many
marked houses (literally so) indicating to the
community of wandering people whether you're
worth a call or not. These folk had quite a
network in the Bradford district, which of course
incorporates many vicarages, manses and other
charitable institutions.

On this particular morning the Reverend Max
Wigley was somewhat puzzled by his visitors. He
was thrown slightly by the presence of a small
child although that wasn't altogether unusual
as 'travelling' families often used their children as emotional weapons to obtain food. But
there seemed to be something different about
this small, pathetic-looking man, something that
didn't quite fit the usual category of such callers.
To start with, he was reasonably clean and
well dressed—but it was his blunt, bold opening
words that made him stand out from others,
'My name is Malcolm Worsley. I'm a criminal
with a long record, and I'm on the run from
a group of men whom I owe a lot of money. I
need your help.'

Max Wigley heard himself inviting them both
into the house. Once seated in the study Malcolm
hid nothing, explaining in detail his criminal
dealings and in particular the events of the
last few weeks leading up to this meeting. The
young vicar sat and listened, quite stunned by
the man's blatant honesty, not a quality usually

attributed to a criminal. Some minutes passed,
and as the tale progressed he began to wonder
where on earth he fitted into this incredible
account, in what possible way he could help
such a man. No sooner had the thought crossed
his mind than he got his answer. 'I need you to fix
up a meeting between me and Margaret so that I
can hand Philip over. It's far too dangerous for
him to stay with me and far too dangerous for
me to go to her. Will you do it, vicar?'

Although Max Wigley had impulsive moments,
he was not in the habit of helping criminals out
of tight spots. So there was nobody more surprised than himself when he realised he'd agreed
with little hesitation to act as 'go-between' for
Malcolm and Margaret. It seemed a simple task,
complicated only by the fact that it needed to
be done quickly. The two men discussed the
details of how, where and when this meeting
could take place.

The church itself seemed good neutral ground,
so the arrangements were made for a 12 noon
meeting. Max agreed to visit Margaret and persuade her to come with him. Malcolm would
return with Philip at the appointed hour. Once
the child was safely in his mother's hands everyone could go his or her own way. As Max Wigley
showed his visitors to the door, he felt confident
that he'd made the right decision.

It wasn't until he settled down at his study
desk again that the doubts started to surface.
Was he aiding a criminal? How could he be sure
that his story was true? His head filled with
niggling questions, and he tried desperately to

justify his position. Surely the child was an innocent victim in it all, and he was quite at liberty to
offer safety and protection to this young life? As
the minutes ticked away, he become less and less
sure about what he had committed himself to, but
he knew that there was no turning back. Max
Wigley respected the trust that had been placed
in his hands, also respecting what seemed to him
a very genuine concern for the welfare of a young
child. He had no intention of breaking a promise
or abusing the trust he had been given; he'd have
to carry out the arrangements as planned.

As the morning went on he became more
and more anxious. His restlessness increased,
and he couldn't settle to work. By this time
he was visualising local newspaper headlines,
'Vicar involved with criminal'. That's all he
needed in the early stages of being vicar of
his first church! Still intent on carrying out his
bargain, he decided some self-protection was in
order just in case something went drastically
wrong. He picked up the telephone and rang
Bradford City Police.

'Is he 5′ 8″, dark haired with a pitted com-
plexion?' came the voice down the 'phone. Max
Wigley assured the detective that this description fitted aptly. What followed confirmed his
inner-most fears and suspicions, and he began
to wish he'd accompanied his wife and children
to the nursery that morning instead of being
available to answer the vicarage door. Warrants
were out for the arrest of Malcolm Worsley in
several counties, but Bradford Police were especially interested in speaking to him about a series

of housebreaking offences. Was he going to be
seeing this man again, the detective asked?

Something within him longed to say 'no'. He
hesitated for some seconds before explaining to
the police exactly what he had agreed to do
and for the child's sake, still intended to do.
Thankfully and to his great relief they appreciated the situation and made it quite clear that
their only concern was picking up Worsley, not
interfering with the arrangements for the child
or his mother. Eventually it was agreed that two
plain clothes policemen would attend the scene,
wait until the handover had taken place and
pick up Malcolm for being in possession of a
stolen vehicle—a charge he would undoubtedly
be guilty of. It seemed a reasonable compromise,
and at least Max Wigley felt he'd kept his bargain
as far as the child was concerned.

His first move was to track down Margaret
on one of the most notorious estates in the
city. The presence of a dog collar caused quite
a stir in the neighbourhood. It wasn't difficult
to find her, but standing on the doorstep persuading her both to believe and agree to the
plans took slightly longer than he had anticipated. Margaret's mother, with whom she shared
a house, objected strongly to the involvement
of the young cleric. She had no time for her
daughter's involvement with Malcolm Worsley,
and it was only concern for young Philip's welfare
that stopped her from telephoning the police
immediately, a decision she later reversed. After
a great deal of persuasion, and much against her
mother's wishes, Margaret agreed, for Philip's

sake, to accompany him at the appropriate time
to the church.

Max Wigley easily spotted the two plain clothes
policemen waiting in a stationary unmarked
vehicle some ten yards down the side street
adjacent to the church. It was seconds before
noon. He felt extremely tense, and Margaret was
far from conversational. She had no idea of the
wider intentions of this meeting, and the vicar
sincerely hoped she never would. He planned to
allow the couple just minutes to exchange words
and most importantly hand over Philip. For the
child's sake it was important to play things down
and get the two of them into his car and away as
quickly as he possibly could. The least he could
do was take them back home again, even if it was
only to convince the disapproving grandmother
that he was trustworthy.

Exactly at noon, he heard the wheels of a
car come suddenly to a halt outside the church
gates. He took a deep breath, looked at Margaret
and turned to walk towards the car. What confronted him was the worst sight he could have
imagined. Just yards in front of them stood a
clearly marked police motor patrol car occupied
by two uniformed men. Its door opened, and a
voice yelled, 'Is 'e 'ere yet, vicar?' Stunned and
extremely angry, Max Wigley bellowed back, 'No,
and he's not likely to be, either, with you sitting
there.' After several seconds of speechlessness
Margaret suddenly found her voice; convinced
she had been used to trap Malcolm, she expressed
her annoyance to the young vicar in no uncertain
terms. Coping with his own anger and trying to

clear the side street of policemen, poor Max tried to calm an understandably annoyed woman. As if all this wasn't enough, yet another police vehicle suddenly pulled up containing two more plain clothes men.

It was now five past twelve and on the street were no fewer than three police vehicles, six policemen of varying rank, Max Wigley, and a very confused Margaret. At that very moment, right at the bottom of the street Malcolm Worsley came round the corner in his stolen green Mini. Without hesitation or consideration of the consequences, Max Wigley ran into the middle of the road waving his arms frantically and shouting 'Get away! The police are here.' Much to his relief the Mini successfully engineered a U-turn, mounting the kerb as it did so, and drove off at great speed up the busy Great Horton Road. Delayed only by the confusion of the situation, two of the police cars followed.

Their chase was unsuccessful as Max Wigley discovered half an hour later when he called in at Odsal Top police station. He hadn't hung around outside the church for explanations or accusations for fear that he might say things he'd later regret. Having safely delivered Margaret to her house he'd had time to calm down and then went in search of the officer responsible for the case. He felt as if it was all a huge fiasco.

It transpired that Margaret's mother had waited until her daughter had left the house, then carried out her threat to ring the police, informing them of the meeting that was about to take place. Unaware of the arrangements made earlier between the vicar and a detective, an officer put out a radio call to all cars in the area to assist in the arrest of Malcolm Worsley. Under normal circumstances the men already assigned to the duty would have responded quickly to the message and assured all concerned that the matter was well in hand. On this occasion, the plain clothes detectives had unfortunately turned off their car radios. Nobody had been more surprised to see two other patrol cars arrive on the scene!

There was little more Max Wigley could do. He was relieved to discover that he wasn't under arrest for aiding and abetting a wanted criminal; and after agreeing to notify the police should Worsley reappear, he was free to leave. As he drove home, he pondered on his day's 'work', wondering which part of his theological training was meant to prepare him for such rich experiences. He could hardly believe it had happened but happily filed it into his memory as one of the more unusual incidents in life that he could always recount to his grandchildren in years to come.

Having put the incident behind him Max turned off the main road into the small side street where his vicarage stood. His mind had already begun to focus on the church council meeting planned for that evening ... until the sight of a green Mini parked alongside the vicarage garden wall gave him a shock. Immediately fearful for his wife and children inside the house, he leapt out of the car and through the front door. Within seconds the door bell rang. Malcolm pushed his way into the house, this time alone, having dumped Philip elsewhere. The same small, pathetic but desperate-looking man pleaded for help. This time he had little success; Max made it clear that the only grounds for help were if Malcolm agreed to give himself up. Much discussion and persuasion took place until yet another meeting was arranged, at the vicarage. Malcolm was to deliver both Philip and himself into the hands of the police, where appropriate action would be taken for both. Malcolm left and Max informed the police.

Not surprisingly, Malcolm failed to keep the appointment.

Four

The Risley Experience

'City police here, vicar. We have one of your flock with us and he's asking to see you.'

It was Malcolm, finally under arrest and claiming his right to one 'phone call. That call wasn't, as is usual, to a solicitor, but to the vicar who had helped him escape from the police two weeks earlier. The sight of Max Wigley standing in the middle of the road waving him away from six policemen had stuck firmly in his mind. Many times since that incident he had wondered exactly what kind of vicar this man was, even if the impact hadn't been sufficient to cause him to return to the vicarage and give himself up as arranged.

It was with mixed emotions that Max Wigley drove to the city police cells. Part of him was thrilled that Malcolm had wanted to see him, but the other part was suspicious of the man's motives, and he could not help wondering if he was the next in line to be conned by this able criminal. By now he had done his homework and learned various information about him from both social and probation services. Everyone he

spoke to had issued the same warnings; 'Have
nothing to do with him. He's a thoroughly bad
person and has hardly been out of prison in ten
years.' Seemingly there were no limits to his
wicked activities, and everyone who had tried
to help had either been robbed or conned in the
process. It seemed that the 'professionals' had
well and truly dumped Malcolm Worsley upon
the rubbish heap of society and perhaps, thought
Max Wigley, with real cause; so he would tread
cautiously.

Clutching a recently published modern trans-
lation of the New Testament (the Good News
Bible), he approached the town hall. He didn't
understand the complexities of a criminal mind
or of the criminal world, but he did know that
the only hope for Malcolm was to be found in the
pages of this paperback book. He felt inadequate
but was determined to explain something of the
new life that could be found in God.

Once Max was inside the cell Malcolm tried
fervently to explain why he had failed to turn up
at the vicarage that day. It was a pathetic tale
and Max, on this occasion, needed little wisdom
to see through the superficial lies and excuses.
It was no surprise to learn that for the last two
weeks Malcolm had simply drifted from place to
place, from pub to pub, acquiring cash one way
or another as he went.

Max sat quietly as Malcolm told of his inner
struggle, the longing to be arrested and yet
lacking the courage to walk into the police station
and give himself up. The end had finally come
that lunch time when two off-duty police officers

had walked into the Queensbury pub where he was mulling over a pint of bitter. He recognised them immediately and knew also that, given the opportunity, they too would recognise him. It seemed the time to end his misery. Approaching them at the bar he had announced without emotion, 'I'm Malcolm Worsley, wanted by the police both here and in Preston. Please take me in.' This was no great achievement in Malcolm's eyes as all he could think of at the time was cutting himself off from the alcohol he so desperately craved and thought he needed. Now, just hours later, he regretted the decision. Sitting locked up in the city cells he felt quite frantic, and the Bradford vicar seemed his only hope.

The tale was followed by all manner of pleas for help and promises of change. Max listened patiently, wanting to believe what he was now hearing. No more crime, no more alcohol, a change of heart, direction, a change of life. How many times had he heard similar determined cries of the heart from folk with far fewer complications in life than Malcolm? He thought how comparatively simple his church members' pastoral problems were and vowed never to complain again about listening to them. Sitting there looking at the bedraggled figure before him he felt momentarily hard and cynical, even unbelieving.

Opening up the New Testament at St John's gospel, chapter 3, he read aloud the story of Nicodemus. Looking Malcolm straight in the eyes he said, 'Malcolm, you must be born again. It is the only way your life and personality can be changed. Jesus is the only person who can do

it. Take this book and read it, for in it you will
find your new life, new direction and hope for
the future.'

It meant little to Malcolm. He looked as confused as Nicodemus had been when Jesus first
spoke those words to him. Malcolm wanted concrete facts and evidence, something he could
hang on to. Max continued to read parts of
the New Testament, this time from Matthew's
gospel, '. . . I tell you not to be worried about
the food and drink you need in order to stay
alive, or about clothes for your body . . . Instead,
be concerned above everything else with the
Kingdom of God and with what he requires
of you, and he will provide you with all these
other things.'

Now *that* he could understand—but whether
he could believe it was another matter. Laughing,
he challanged Max, 'What? God provide me with
food, drink and clothes? You've got to be kidding
me, vicar! Will he provide me with a house too?
No God can do that sort of thing!'

The vicar could see the seeming absurdity of
it all from Malcolm's viewpoint, yet he knew it
was the truth. God could change this man's life,
set him upon a new track and provide him with
more than he could ever need or desire. But it
was his choice, his decision, and nobody could do
it for him.

Before leaving he slipped an address card into
the cover of the New Testament and handed
it to Malcolm. He told him he would pray for
him every day, asking God to bring him to
repentance and faith in Jesus. For the third

time in two weeks Max Wigley said goodbye
without knowing if he'd ever see or hear from
this man again.

It wasn't difficult to get a signed statement
from a man like Malcolm. Two detectives escorted
him across the Pennines and back to Preston,
where the earlier police warrant had been put
out for his arrest. En route they stopped at
a moorside pub and filled him with alcohol
until he signed their prepared statement. At
that stage of alcohol withdrawal he would have
signed anything for a drink.

Once in Preston the routine was all too familiar.
He occupied a station cell until called by the
magistrate, who refused bail and ordered him
to Risley Remand Centre. There was never any
question of bail for Malcolm; he knew no one was
prepared to risk money for his sake.

Risley, or 'Grisley Risley' as the inmates called
it, was a purpose-built top security prison where
criminals of every description came and went,
each awaiting their court appearance and sentence. It was a grey, concrete, soulless building
and emotions ran high as anxious first-time
petty offenders lived nervously alongside sea-
soned criminals.

Malcolm's memories of these short-term con-
finements in this and other prisons were not
good. One vivid and particularly painful occasion
was back in 1960 in Walton, Liverpool—the last
hanging of a British criminal—an occasion that
went down in history. It wasn't the kind of
experience he ever wanted to remember, yet it
was one that he could never forget.

Such executions always took place in the morning, and no man was allowed out of his cell on that day. Prison officers walked around under a black cloud of silence that brought gloom and doom to the whole building, until the appointed hour when the hanging took place. Then slowly and gradually each man would take his metal drinking mug and strike up a slow rhythm of banging against his cell door. This protest death chant of mugs gathered more and more participants until the whole building vibrated with the dirge of death. Sometimes it continued for hours, no man daring not to join in for fear of his fellow prisoners. The heaviness remained throughout the long hours of the day, dying away only in the darkness of the night.

Malcolm knew that this was one experience that he would never have to live through again, for which he was deeply grateful. But Risley he still did have to face, plus his court hearing and the inevitable sentence. Only one thing was different on this occasion: the New Testament that went with him.

He started by reading the gospels, some parts of which he remembered from his days at Sunday school as a child. But for Malcolm by far the most interesting and fascinating section of the New Testament was the Book of the Acts of the Apostles. He read and reread it tirelessly, not just once but sometimes six or seven times a day, every day of the week. There was something about the life of St Paul that captivated him. Saul (later called Paul) was responsible for keeping the Christians in order, suppressing

their new found faith and preventing them from
preaching and teaching about Jesus Christ. He
regularly ordered men and women from their
homes into prison and stood by watching the
stoning of Stephen, the first Christian martyr.
Yet this same man, only months later, was himself imprisoned for speaking about the same
faith as those he had persecuted. Malcolm was
intrigued. What had brought about such a drastic
change in this man's life, and was it possible that
his own life might change to the same degree? He
read on in search of the answer to his questions.
Reading the Bible came a lot easier than praying.
Gripped though he was by the life and journeys of
St Paul, he didn't always know in his own mind
who or what God was. Despite all he was reading
and wanting to believe, there were still moments
when he even doubted the existence of a God.
He remembered how Max Wigley had told him
to pray, to speak to God and ask his forgiveness,
but he struggled desperately, wanting something
or someone to focus his prayers on. Out of sheer
desperation and determination he looked up at
the light bulb and spoke aloud, 'Dear God, Max
Wigley says if I ask, you will help. I don't know
who or what you are, so I'm speaking to the light
bulb. I don't know if this will work but I'm going
to try. I'm going to keep on reading this book, and
I promise to keep looking for the answers. I've
nothing to lose.'

Day after day the Bible reading continued, and
the same prayer was repeated, always directed
towards the light bulb. By now Malcolm was
mapping out the missionary journeys of St Paul,

drawing his information not only from the Book of Acts but from all Paul's letters to the early churches. He was not satisfied until every detail fell into place.

It was while he was searching for an answer to what he thought was an inconsistent teaching in the New Testament that, for the first time, he sensed the living presence of God in his cell. He spoke to God. 'Come on, God, what does this mean? I don't understand, surely there is something amiss here? Please show me what I need to know.' There was no immediate answer to his question, no voice from heaven, yet the silence had been broken. At that precise moment God had broken through the roof, through the light bulb, and was with him in the cell. Malcolm knew he had just spoken to a *person*. The question drifted into insignificance, for what he was experiencing was far greater and more important than any question. God was there. *God was there*. The words went round and round inside him. He couldn't see him or touch him, but there was no doubt that he was there. He hardly dare move for fear that this visitor might go away. It was overwhelming. Finally he managed to sit on the edge of his bed, bowed his head and spoke: 'Lord God, I know you're real, here, right now. Please, please, let Jesus help me just as he did Paul.' It was only the beginning. Praying, he discovered, brought him into the presence of God in a way he had never experienced before. He could talk to him just as if he were a person standing in the same room. And the conversations became two-way. But God didn't use human words. His presence spoke of power, holiness and a purity that was quite foreign to Malcolm. He sat for long periods of time feeding on the stillness and learning to sense something of the vast and awesome nature of this God.

As he sat in the silence images came into his mind; pictures of his past and in particular of the crimes he had committed. They were painful reminders of the criminal mind and deeds that had dominated the last ten years. Watching them flash past his mind's eye, in the presence of God, was agonising.

Every picture varied, but rarely was there a time when they didn't appear. One was especially painful. It took him back to a day he had burgled a small terraced house in broad daylight. Having successfully broken into a gas meter and confident that the way was clear, he made a swift exit through the rear garden of the house. He had not seen the small fair haired girl standing behind the garden wall. Therefore he almost ran into her when pulling open the back gate. For a brief moment he hesitated, unsure of what to say or do. There were only the two of them in the back alley and he needed to move quickly so he resorted to shouting down at the child in a loud threatening voice. He was some yards away before he dare turn round to see the effects of his booming words and it was this picture that had surfaced in his mind's eye now. A petrified three year old stood paralysed by fear, eyes filled with tears that were about to flood her pale cheeks. She was lifting a finger to the corner of an eye and taking a deep breath ready to scream.

The image haunted Malcolm and wouldn't leave him until he looked the child in the eye and faced up to the pain that he had put her through. Only when he was full of disgust and shame for his action did the picture stop coming. It was the start of a long process which made him face up to the realities of all he had done.

Day after day he begged God to take away the horrendous pictures of himself that were now flooding his mind day and night. He tried to stop praying in the hope that they would disappear, but it was no good. 'God, I'm sorry,' he repeated over and over again, desperate to be forgiven. But he could find no peace. All God seemed to be saying was, 'No you're not, Malcolm. You don't know what being sorry is. Look and remember all you have done. You did those things, Malcolm. You're guilty of all that'. Malcolm retorted, 'I *am* sorry, *really* sorry, I didn't mean to do them.' The more he cried, the more God showed him his wretchedness; every single sin of his life came to the surface and he was forced to look at them all. The torture was unbearable, the pain unrelenting, and he could stand it no longer. He felt there was no future. Life couldn't go on in this state.

By now he was drifting around in a state of semi-consciousness, not having slept for several weeks. Tears streamed permanently from his eyes, and he spent hours of the day curled up under his bunk in an attempt to hide from himself and God. He'd always prayed sat or curled in a tight ball on his bed. For some reason this particular night he sensed God telling him to get on his knees. Already totally humiliated and unable to face himself, he considered this final act of submission impossible. He had nothing else to say or do before God. How could he ask him to go on his knees in that state? The answer was a definite 'No', but the niggling request returned throughout the night as he tossed and turned in his bunk. As the early hours of the morning approached, in desperation, to end the torture inside, Malcolm fell onto his knees at the side of his bunk and prayed what he was sure would be his last prayer: 'OK God, you win. I am the worst person who ever lived. I know I'll never get into your kingdom. I'm too bad. I deserve nothing. I'm worse than Paul. I admit it, so now leave me alone. Let me get on with my life. Just leave me alone.'

Returning to his bunk feeling confident he'd finally got God out of his system, Malcolm slept longer and more deeply than he had done in weeks. No more scenes from the past flashing through his mind or recurring nightmares. No tossing and turning in his bunk. It was pure, blissful, childlike sleep. The battle was over, and God had won.

A new day dawned, and a new man awoke. Aware that he had slept for the first time in weeks he stood up a little bemused, struggling to recall the events of the night. Everything had changed: the cell, the air that he breathed, his body—absolutely everything about him and around him was different. He took a deep breath, his chest expanding inches further than it had ever done before. He felt lighter and warm; the

air had a freshness and vitality in it that he'd
never previously known. Inside he felt clean and
pink, new and special. Like a mother examining
her new baby, he stared at his arms and legs and
counted the fingers on his hands. The sky looked
blue; the sun blazed through the tiny window.

It was as if a surgeon had taken a scalpel and
removed the past, once and for all. An enormous
weight had been lifted from his shoulders and
dumped somewhere along the Damascus Road.
His torture had ended in that final admission
and submission to God. Now he understood what
had happened to St Paul all those years ago, and
the same thing had happened to him. It was all
God's doing, none of his own. The past had been
wiped out. He was forgiven, and he knew he had
a place in heaven along with his hero Paul. It was
indescribable.

As he stood locked in his cell, Malcolm Worsley
realised that this was a freedom far greater than
he had ever experienced before. He had met with
a God of new beginnings, of new birth and hope.
His searching had come to an end, yet somehow
he knew that his new life had only just begun.

Five

Letters From Prison

The Risley experience had been powerful and unforgettable. Even Malcolm struggled to believe the change in himself. For the first time in years he wanted to laugh out loud and run around like a child let loose in a sunny garden. The sunshine came from within and shone out through his eyes and smile; his garden was the cell, corridors and canteen. It left prison officers and cell mates puzzled but undisturbed. They were quite sure that whatever experience he had had, religious or otherwise, it would not have any lasting effect. Prison life succeeded in squashing anything that might be remotely good or positive.

Malcolm knew it would take time to prove just how different he was. So far it had been an experience that even he hadn't fully grasped. Actually explaining it to others seemed impossible. He simply felt different and knew that he was no longer carrying around a lifetime's guilt. Couldn't others see it? How was he meant to put that sense of relief and freedom into words? They ridiculed him tirelessly at first, but their scorn was like water off a duck's back.

Nobody was going to take away this wonderful experience; as far as Malcolm was concerned, it was there to stay.

Exactly how he was going to walk those first few steps at the start of his new life he didn't know. He felt like a newborn baby. There was no midwife or parent to spoon or bottle-feed him; no one to catch him when he fell or bathe the cuts and bruises when he was hurting. But Malcolm had every intention of trying with or without the help. The last few weeks (and years!) had been hell, and now he had had a taste of heaven that no one was going to take from him.

There was only one person in the world to whom Malcolm felt able to turn: Max Wigley. He was his only friend, the only non-criminal he knew. Everybody else had long since given up on him and would be unlikely to believe any further tales or explanations about his latest good intentions. But Malcolm knew he had to earn his right to speak, to convince this vicar he was sincere in his search for faith. He tried very hard to impress upon him the fact that he was a genuine seeker. The first of many letters read:

Dear Mr Wigley
You may be surprised to know that I have made a point of reading the New Testament you gave me for at least an hour a day. The gospels although similar in their accounts of Christ's life I found very interesting and enjoyable. The Acts of the Apostles was probably to me the more stimulating. It has been these last three days, when I have been reading Paul's

letter to the Romans and Corinthians, that I have found it rather heavy going. I am going to try and contact the chaplain here to see if he has a booklet helping people to understand these letters more clearly. In the meantime I am rereading St Luke.

You mentioned in your letter that you would try and get someone to come and see me. If you could arrange this, I would be most grateful. There is no limit to the amount of visits we have and they are daily (except Sundays) between 1.30 pm and 4 pm.

Freedom is nothing until you lose it. A lot of people don't even appreciate what freedom is, myself included. I honestly and sincerely pray to God that there will be a solution to my way of life. I am most grateful for your encouragement so far, and if I can mention part of St Matthew's gospel, it proves to me that people are prepared to help. The passage I have in mind is chapter 25 verses 31-46. These verses show that God has no time for hypocrisy and only those who carry on their lives in a true manner are acceptable in God's eyes.

I reread St John's gospel again as you said. Chapter 3 was a great help. Tonight I will be reading the letter from James. I hope to hear from you soon.

All the best. Yours sincerely, Malcolm

Malcolm wrote as often as his prison allowance allowed him to buy stamps. It was always once, sometimes twice or even three times a week. The replies were not as frequent as he would have

liked, and at the early stages of their correspondence Max expressed great caution in his writing.
Despite his daily prayers for Malcolm, he still had
to be sure that he wasn't being taken for a ride.
Early in their relationship he wrote:

Dear Malcolm
Thank you for your letters. By now you should
have received my letter, plus stamps and pen.

I was thrilled to bits that you had read the
New Testament I gave you. As you say, the
books of the Romans and Corinthians are
heavy going unless you have something to help
you understand the background to the books.
But press on and perhaps you are right to
reread Luke's gospel as such an understanding
of Jesus and his ministry is essential to finding
him as your own Saviour and Lord.

There is only one solution to your way of life
as it is, and that is Jesus Christ. There is no
other way for a person to be changed, only in
the power of God. From the probation service
and other people I know your background very
well now, Malcolm. I want to help by writing
to you, but don't try to con me; I'm the wrong
sort. If you sincerely want help to find a new
way of life, then I will help you by pointing you
to Christ. But if I find you are conning me, I'm
afraid we will part company.

I have found that you have lied to me about
several matters or perhaps not told me the
whole truth with the intent of deceiving. You
have a reputation to live down, and it is only
God who can help you to do it. Your letters

themselves are deep and interesting and it is
obvious that you are interested in the subject
of the Lord Jesus. It is not a matter of me
trusting you but of you proving to me that
you can be trusted. I certainly want to give
you every opportunity. I continue to pray for
you daily that you might find new life in Christ
and the strength and power to begin again.

Best regards, Max Wigley

Max had never been so involved with helping a
criminal before. He was anxious to do and say
the right things but at the same time realised
that he was perhaps naive and inexperienced in
relating to such people. Friends had been keen to
offer him all sorts of advice, much of which had
been based on their own negative experiences. It
would have been easier to dismiss Malcolm as
'not his problem', but something within spurred
him on in his writing. By now members of his
congregation had joined him in praying daily for
this convict.

He was very careful at first to resist the temptation to respond to Malcolm's continual pleading
to visit him in Risley. The letters and requests
came thick and fast, and although the distance
was not too great he decided to restrict his contact
to letters. It seemed in the circumstances the best
way to test this man's sincerity.

Over the weeks Malcolm's letters changed
from constant attempts to prove himself to more
subdued reflection on his circumstances and
future. This was the first real indication to

Max that he was facing the realities of his situation and serious about living a Christian life. It wasn't too long before he faced his first real test. His court hearing date was fast approaching, and he was dreading its outcome. He reflected upon his position and the likely sentence in a letter to Max:

Dear Mr Wigley

It is not long until I appear in court. I wish I could think that some alternative to plain prison would be given to me, but I think it most unlikely. Turning everyone against me as I have done over the last couple of months has really sealed my coffin. To get the courts to offer to help you to reform needs support, and I have nobody at the moment. Over the past few weeks I have been wondering what I could say in way of mitigation to the recorder when I appear before him. So many thoughts and ideas have passed through my mind, but in the end, it all boils down to one thing. I am guilty, and nothing I nor anyone else can say can alter the fact. All I hope for is that the recorder will find the answer to me, somewhere in the reports he will have on me.

At least prison will give me time to study my Bible and perhaps I can use it to shield against 'nick' talk. I was beginning to think that the church as a whole was just like the prison church, but since you gave me the Bible to read I can see that it isn't. I'd have never thought to look for God in this place if

I hadn't come to the vicarage that day about
ten weeks ago now.

Best wishes, Malcolm.

Considering the circumstances, Malcolm thought
it unlikely he would receive anything less than
a two-and-a-half to three-year sentence for his
crime, so the news of twenty-one months felt
to him a miracle. It was the chance he needed
to stop and take stock of all that had happened
in the previous few months; the chance to set
himself realistic targets and hit them. As much
as he would have loved to have walked free from
the courts that day, he knew he had a price to
pay for his crime and needed time to work at
his new-found faith before being let loose into
the world again. Soon he started his sentence in
Liverpool jail.

As well as the help given by Max Wigley in his
letters, books became a most valuable source of
encouragement for him in these first few stages
of growth. The prison library was extremely
limited but did provide a little stimulation for
this enquiring mind. Study had never been his
favourite pastime; in fact he couldn't remember
the last time he had actually read a book—perhaps while still at school nearly fifteen years ago.
But now he was searching out all the reading
matter that he could find to keep this renewed
mind alive.

In the prison library, mixed in with thrill-
ers and western stories, Malcolm found various
translations of the Bible which he delighted in

comparing with each other. He sat daily with three or four versions open at the same passage comparing the words and phrases. Numerous questions surfaced in his mind and were automatically directed at Max, whose time was increasingly spent ploughing through theological texts in an attempt to produce the answers. The questions seemed endless.

How many modern translations were there, and how did they differ from each other? Was it wise to have so many different 'interpretations' of the same story? Was Luke one of Paul's converts, and if so why was it that he was able to write so accurately of Jesus' life and teachings, since Paul was converted after the death of Christ? Could it be that Mark and Luke had met and discussed their writings? What about the various source documents? Why was it that the Old Testament seemed complicated?

Malcolm's insatiable thirst for learning had replaced a thirst for alcohol. He had moved from self-destruction to the rebuilding of his body, mind and spirit. Contact with prison chaplains from the various denominations (always failing to see the need for such divisions) provided further channels for study. On arriving at Liverpool he enrolled on his first Bible study course and signed up for the weekly study class with a few other prisoners. His understanding and confidence grew fast until, instead of asking numerous questions in his letters to Max, they became an account of all that he had learned that week. And his sense of fun and humour emerged too:

Dear Mr Wigley

I have been waiting all week to be able to buy a stamp so that I can write to you and apologise for not spotting your deliberate mistake sooner. As you will know from my last two letters I spent a great deal of my time during my last week at Risley studying the Resurrection, and it was not until I got here that I continued again with Paul. By the way, if your reference of Acts 4:4 is not a deliberate mistake might I suggest 500 lines? As to whether Luke was ever in Colossae I would not like to say, but I do know that Paul never went there, even though he must have been quite near on a number of occasions.

The church at Colossae was probably started by Epaphroditus, who was later imprisoned in Rome with Paul. Paul's only contact with the church there was through his letter to them from Rome, probably in prison in 62 AD. I don't know whether you are looking for some indication from me that I am indeed studying the gospels and epistles.

After all, isn't Paul proof of the living church? A persecutor turned preacher. I cannot get away from the power and strength behind his preaching. What a wonderful experience it must have been that gave him the courage to overcome several beatings, whippings, a stoning, shipwrecks and imprisonment. The sufferings of the early apostles is proof beyond doubt that it was something more than mortal they were fighting for.

I have found a couple of verses which I read

every day. They are in Paul's letter to the
Ephesians, 4:28-32, beginning 'He who has
been stealing must steal no longer, but must
work, doing something useful with his own
hands ...' I have also been trying to read
a book by Father Herbert on the Christian
community, but all it has taught me so far
is that modern church politics is best left
alone. There are so many divisions in the
Christian church that some are almost like
different religions.

Best wishes, Malcolm.

The study continued intensively, encouraged by
Max's regular letters and by this time an occasional visit from Bradford. These visits meant a
great deal to Malcolm, more than he could ever
express in words. He had a friend who wasn't a
criminal, someone he could trust and rely upon
for support and encouragement. He kept every
letter received from Max, reading and rereading
them daily in his cell. Along with his Bible they
were fast becoming his lifeline, without which he
knew he would sink.

Dear Malcolm
Thank you for your last two letters. I'm sorry
I put the wrong text when referring to Luke
knowing Paul; it should have been Colossians
4:4 and not Acts 4:4. I assure you it wasn't a
deliberate mistake. I'm thrilled you are learning so quickly about your scriptures. Of course,

head knowledge is important, but heart knowledge is most important. We can know all about theology without knowing Christ as a living person in our lives.

Don't worry, Malcolm, I'm not trying to trip you up. It's obvious from your letters that you are really studying the scriptures and that you have great potential in the academic sense. If you went to night school and got stuck in you would very soon find yourself with some good qualifications. I'm glad to hear that you're getting stuck into the Bible study class. I haven't read the book you mentioned but it's obviously very interesting. Anyway, I'd better close Malcolm. Please keep writing. Although I cannot write as frequently as you, I will endeavour to answer your letters when I can. I continue to remember you in prayer and pray that you might find Christ as a person who can forgive your past, give you power to live the life you want now and give you certainty in a world that has none.

With best wishes, Max.

The new life that Malcolm had found in Christ was changing everything. He fought daily to bring his body, mind and spirit under the influence and control of God's Holy Spirit, yet he was never under any illusion as to the real opposition he faced. His life was modelled on that of his hero St Paul. If Paul could endure such hardships in the power of God, so could Malcolm, or at least he was determined to try.

The one thing they both had in common was their experience of prison.

Grateful though he was for the opportunity for learning, he knew even at this early stage of his stay in prison that the ultimate test would come at the end of his sentence. He never stopped wondering if his faith would be strong enough when that time came and openly expressed his fears and concerns about this:

Dear Max

Sometimes I feel that imprisonment isn't hard on a person. It deprives him of his liberty, but that's all. The punishment part of a sentence doesn't start until you are RELEASED! This is when you have to face society with £4 in your pocket and a blank insurance card. On top of this, you have a record (for the rest of your life), and therefore your choice of jobs is limited. I'm not saying it is impossible to live down a past, because I would be lying; but it is made difficult by the red tape that ties together our legal and aftercare system. I think that's enough backbiting for one letter and anyway I'm sure that you are aware of these 'practical' problems.

Spiritual problems are another matter, and particularly your reference to a heart experience with Jesus Christ. At the time of writing I am fully aware that Jesus Christ lives in the world today and can forgive us our sins. I want to be honest with you, Max, and at the same time be honest with myself. I would like to believe here and now that I will come out

of prison a God-fearing Christian, and I pray
to our Lord Jesus Christ every night that this
will happen. But locked away in here it is quite
easy to lose all perspective of reality. As you
know we live behind an eighteen foot wall in
a closed community and therefore there are no
social temptations. Was it Karl Marx who said,
'religion is the opiate of the masses'? This is
how it appears to work in here from what
I've been told. You are not faced with the
temptations of a modern society and therefore
there is little scope for sinning. In a situation
like this it is quite easy to kid ourselves that
we have found Christ and that religion is
the answer. Of course it *is* the answer and
the only answer, but will this environmental
acceptance of Christ stay with us when we
are released? Or will it, like an opiate, wear
off? I have thought a lot about this and I feel
I would be cheating on you if I did not mention
it. I feel 99.9999% sure that the feeling I have
in my heart for Christ is a lasting one. I know
what it means to love, to care for people and to
understand the glorious sacrifice that Christ
made for us. I feel stronger and stronger every
day that Christ can make something of me. I
feel a lot happier now than I have in a long
time and really when you think about it I have
no 'practical' reason to be.

By the way, the second letter of Paul's to
the Corinthians—was the last chapter written
by Paul? The rest of the letter although jerky
in parts is a very moving and sincere epistle,
but the last chapter seems completely out of

context. I'd be grateful for your comments,
but don't neglect the important business to
write to me.

With best wishes through Christ, Malcolm.

Max Wigley was hopeful that Malcolm would
remain in Liverpool for the rest of his sentence
as he had reason to visit the city regularly and so
could call at the prison. He also knew a number
of clergymen in the area who would do the same.
But it wasn't to be. By the middle of January
1971 Malcolm had been sent to Haverigg in
Cumbria to serve the remaining ten months at
this open prison. It was isolated, bleak, and very
difficult to reach. Max thought it unlikely that
he would ever find the opportunity to travel so
far and so decided that, apart from their written
correspondence, he had to find someone else to
encourage and visit Malcolm during these critical
months. Will Barker, a Scripture Union worker,
became that person.

Six

Haverigg

Will Barker had considerable experience working with offenders, especially youngsters who had been sent to approved schools and borstals. Over the years he had grown to understand something of the problems faced by these young people, especially the struggle they encountered trying to earn a place back in society after a period of time inside institutions of this kind. Occasionally his work took him into prisons where the problems were even greater, intensified by repeated failure and rejection by society. Will had a deep concern for these boys and men and longed for them to find a new beginning with God and in the world at large. His life was dedicated to that task.

The invitation from Max Wigley to visit Malcolm inside Haverigg delighted him. There was no greater joy to him than nurturing a new Christian in the faith, knowing the opposition he would find inside prison. Will was determined to do all he could to encourage this man, so their first meeting was arranged soon after Malcolm's arrival.

'Will,' Malcolm said, 'Can I tell you how I met Jesus?' For the next fifty minutes he relayed his

story to the transfixed Will Barker, who neither
spoke nor moved as he listed to the tale. Never
before had he met anyone quite so free and
yet confined within the prison walls. In all his
years of ministry among offenders he had never
encountered such a powerful testimony as this.
He saw quite clearly the impact of God upon
this man's life and began to sense the privilege
he now had in helping him on this journey of
faith. As Will drove away from Haverigg later
that day he wondered who had benefited most
from the visit, himself or Malcolm? It was the
first of many and the foundation of what was to
become a close, affectionate relationship.

There was little doubt that Malcolm would
need Will's support in the days ahead, despite
his bubbly enthusiasm at the start. Haverigg
brought him a lot of 'stick' from cell mates
and fellow prisoners. He wasn't surprised as it
was common practice for newcomers to be 'put
through the mill', and he knew the routine well.
But now, as a Christian, he expected it to be
far worse—and he was right. He braced himself,
willing to suffer for the sake of Jesus Christ
and eager at all times to follow the example
of his hero St Paul. His only guideline was the
New Testament, and from what he had read he
understood that every Christian should expect
persecution of some kind; therefore he should
take his in a spirit of rejoicing, glad he was
considered worthy of such suffering.

These experiences so early on in his Christian
life served to strengthen his faith and make him
determined to keep going, whatever the cost. As

the weeks went by his desire to speak about what God had done for him increased. He took every opportunity he could.

'The prison,' he wrote to Max, 'is run on the basis of an army camp, inside a wire enclosure. Mountains and hills swell up around us, a bleak but beautiful sight. Inside the wire we live fairly well. We have a choice at meal times, and the beds are clean and comfortable. I told the welfare officer that I have put all my problems into God's hands. He is a Jehovah's Witness, so I thought it wise not to mention that I am a dedicated blood donor!'

A sense of humour was so important on the 'inside', and Malcolm tried hard to show his fellow prisoners that life under lock and key needn't be unbearable. Of course they were not convinced that the newcomer had anything of value to offer them and proceeded to amuse themselves at his expense. He became the object of name-calling, ridicule and pranks, especially the ones that risked his getting into trouble with prison officers. Malcolm remained philosophical and unwavering in his faith, knowing that only time and continued good example would silence their laughter. As he saw it, many wanted to talk about God but were simply too embarrassed to do so. He explained to Max:

There is an odd lad who continues to have a go at me, but really I don't mind, and I can turn it to my advantage. They usually greet me with 'Good morning vicar', cross themselves, and tell me that this 'God jazz' is no good, and that it is the brainchild of a con man. As I see it, with no encouragement from me they are speaking about God, and I want them to talk more about him. This only serves to remind me that my every minute and action should be worthy of him who gave up his life for me. Paul was obviously influenced by the tremendous faith of Stephen, who forgave all his persecutors in his final prayer. I too must withstand this persecution, in love for these men.

The men became Malcolm's priority, his first mission field as an evangelist. He felt deep compassion for them all, knowing full well the gap between a criminal and a Christian, and longing for them to experience the love and forgiveness he had found in Christ, the new life that he was now living. As time went on, they couldn't fail to notice the difference in him; and despite their provoking and abuse, many asked Malcolm to tell them how he had found God. There seemed hardly a day when he didn't have an audience of one kind or another. He took these opportunities seriously, working out how he could clearly explain what had happened to him and encourage others to seek the same thing. He shared many of these times with Max:

I tried to tell Joe, Pete, Steve, Tony, Ray and Bob how I came to know God and was surprised at how difficult I found it to explain. Thinking about it afterwards, I decided it all comes down to two things. Firstly we have to WANT God to help us; and secondly we have to BELIEVE God can help us. I know I experienced difficulty praying to God because I did not know him. But I asked Jesus to help me over this even though I didn't know him at the time, either. It is surprising that if we pray to God and tell him that, even though we don't know what he is or where he is—He will help us.

Malcolm had his work cut out answering all the questions fired at him by the men. Some were sincere, genuine searching questions, and others were thrown out to trick and trip him. 'Why,' one man asked, 'was my father maimed in a work accident, crippled and continually in pain for life?' Another wanted to know why, if Jesus could still a stormy sea, did God allow church steeples to be struck by lightning? How Malcolm struggled with convincing the Jewish prisoners of the Messiahship of Christ. Even his personal exposition of the book of Hebrews and an outline of Old Testament prophecy didn't appear to help.

All of his free time was now centred on bringing these men to a knowledge and experience of Christ. It was a slow process, but in time he began to see the fruits of his labour. Informal discussions in the cells became organised groups and Bible studies, and Malcolm's companions boosted the numbers at every denominational service in the prison. It was unimportant to him as to how people worshipped, as long as the message of Jesus was preached. There were however moments of great frustration when, in his eyes,

the services failed to communicate anything of
lasting value to the convicts. In desperation one
day he poured out his woes to Max:

I have been wondering again this past week
or two whether there is something wrong with
my outlook on Christianity. I believe we should
preach Jesus by keeping our faith simple.
Christ is the church and the doorway to eternal
life. I believe that the Holy Spirit is a MUST in
all our services here. I firmly believe that if we
hand over the meeting to him and have faith,
he will work among us. Then who can doubt
his influence? I prayed really hard for the
numbers to increase, and through the power
of the Holy Spirit working in and among us,
the numbers rose. Our meetings have gone
well when we have spoken of the new life
offered through Christ Jesus, but once again
this week the numbers are down. Why? The
chaplain has gone all 'choral' again. Why in
the name of all I believe in will he not allow
the Holy Spirit to use all of us to bring Christ
into these services? Hymns are very nice and I
enjoy singing, but can Catholics, Pentecostals
and Methodists sing to Anglican chants?
Honestly Max I begin to wonder whether I've
got the message back to front. I dearly love our
Lord, and if I sound pious it is only because
I really and truly do believe in Jesus Christ
the Saviour of mankind. I reach boiling point
sometimes when lads come up to me and say
they are not going any more because it is all
singing. I work hard for the Lord, and I love

every minute of it, but it really gets me down
when men are keeping away because we are
NOT preaching the gospel. It's ridiculous—or
is it just my problem, Max?'

He compensated for the lack of preaching in the
chapel by sharing even more with cell mates,
especially those who were slow to read or write.
'Tell us the stories of Jesus,' they'd ask, 'in
your own words.' Malcolm spent hours relating
the familiar New Testament stories, sometimes
reading them directly from his now tattered Good
News Bible. He taught them how to pray, when
to pray, and what to pray for. Many came to him
asking him to pray with them or for them, and
some committed their lives to Christ during that
time. Pete was one such man.
    During free time one day Pete come to talk
to Malcolm about a matter that concerned him
greatly. He had received a visit from his wife,
who had told him that the electricity was due
to be cut off the following day if she didn't
pay the bill. She had no source of income; Pete
had none, and she and the children were likely
to freeze without heat and light or source of
cooking. He felt helpless and extremely anxious.
The burden weighed heavily, especially as he
wanted deperately as a new Christian to do
right by his wife. Malcolm read to him the part
of Matthew's gospel that Max had read to him
that day in the Bradford cell about God providing
all our needs. They then prayed together. Having
given the whole matter over to God, Pete left.
    Some days later he came running up to Malcolm

clutching a letter from his wife. As she had been walking down the street the day following her visit to prison, an old friend of Pete's stopped and gave her some money he had owed him from some time ago. It was enough to pay the bill and buy food for the children. Malcolm and Pete worked out that the incident had occurred at the precise time of their praying together.

Pete was overjoyed and spent the rest of the day telling his friends that God had provided for his family in a miraculous way. A couple of days later he reappeared at Malcolm's door with Keith, another inmate, and the request, 'Malcolm, will you pray with Keith? He has debts of £250!' After Malcolm had explained that the gospel and prayer was a little more than simply praying for money, Keith got his prayer.

As time went on Malcolm received great strength and fellowship from his new converts. Will Barker was now visiting not only Malcolm but several of the men who had received Christ as their Saviour. He brought into the prison Christian films for them to watch and books for those who could read, but above all he prayed for them and with them. The discussion groups grew and became a recognised and established part of prison life for many of the men in Haverigg. Between them, Malcolm, Will and Max linked up prisoners with local church ministers and members in their home town ready for when they got out. Malcolm recognised the help and support that he had gained from Max and was eager to see every man given this opportunity.

Not all who attended the group meetings were

believers, but everyone would contribute to the
many and varied topics of discussion. Mindful
always of the need for these men one day to live
in the outside world, Malcolm's view of life and
choice of discussion topics was never restricted
just to prison.

Max regularly fed him with details of current
affairs, especially national concerns, ranging
from the killing of Liverpool policemen to North-
ern Ireland; disaster in Pakistan to more local
events such as his own parish mission. The
men held regular prayer meetings for this Bradford church and made sure that all denominational services in the prison were praying for
it.

As the sentence dragged on Malcolm found life
on the inside a struggle. He loved witnessing
and sharing with the men, but not all of them
were quite so determined as him to keep the
faith. There were weeks when he felt he was
moving backwards, not forwards. The ridicule
from others was unrelenting and a sense of
helplessness came over him as he fought to keep
his brothers in Christ on the right track. 'How
I wish I were more experienced in the ways of
God!' he cried to Max, adding, 'Do you ever get
impatient with God? I've been praying for a particular answer for weeks now, but still nothing.'

There were darker times to come. He feared the
time when he would be released and the problems
that would inevitably follow. While he was on the
inside, alcohol had ceased to be a problem; but he
knew he had to face both it and the outside world
in the near future. The closer that time came,

the darker he felt his world was becoming, lying under an overcasting shadow that seemed to be growing by the day. He wrote:

Being an alcoholic or being aware of being an alcoholic is the main thing I have come to accept during this sentence. It was Christ who showed me my weakness and made me aware of the consequences of kidding myself about it. Alcoholism is a disease. The thinking processes of the brain are affected by alcohol in the blood system. This is known as 'alcoholic thinking'. I was thinking alcoholic when I called on you, Max, and though I have now been dry for almost eleven months, occasionally I still think alcoholic. Does this surprise you? I have been pickled in alcohol for years, and during that time my thinking did a complete flip. But, thanks to the grace of God, it has been reversed again, and I am back to my pre-alcoholic way of thinking. I don't know if this is difficult for you to understand. An alcoholic always procrastinates in everything, whether it be a decision or action. Nobody can know just how dark an alcoholic's world is unless he has been there. But I have come out of the darkness and was faced with the Living Light. Christ is the light of the world, but to me the most important word is TRUTH, or honesty. Honesty with myself, honesty with others, but—more important—with God. Honesty and alcoholism are opposites. The light comes when I acknowledge Christ. The truth comes because I walk in the light and the way

becomes easier because I walk in light and
truth. Perhaps this may help you understand
me a bit better.

Malcolm might well have been free of alcohol,
but other temptations still came his way inside
Haverigg. His earnings were small, but he was
able at times to save for a few allowed luxuries.
The small group of those who met to study
and pray would also give regularly to charitable
concerns through the prison chaplains. The total
amount may have only been pence but Malcolm
nonetheless considered giving a good principle
for them to all adopt inside, in the hope that
it might continue when they got out. His own
downfall on money matters came as a particular
blow to him which he grieved over and confessed
in another letter to Max:

I will start this letter before I lose the urge to
tell you of the stupid weakness I succumbed
to without even thinking. Just before I moved
into my single room I decided that the best
thing I could do with some of my money was
to buy a Bible, as the one you gave me is now
held together with a couple of rolls of sellotape.
Then I was told that I could have a radio in this
room. So what did I do? I signed over £4.25 and
bought a transistor. It wasn't until I had it in
my room that I realised what a weak fool I
am. Even this confession doesn't help much
because it doesn't alter the fact that I fell into
one of the devil's simplest traps. I know I
should have used this money to pay back some

of what I've stolen. I wish sometimes, wrongly of course, that God didn't prick my conscience so much. Perhaps this will show you what a bad example of Christianity I am, but on the brighter side with God's help I try harder to be a better person.

The tension in Malcolm increased as the time for his release approached. He knew his faith was real, and he wanted desperately to continue to walk in God's way. Release would be the biggest test of all, for the failures of the past hung over him like a dark cloud. He knew there had been many occasions when he had genuinely sought work and tried to build up normal, healthy relationships, but everything had gone against him. Why, he feared, should things be any different on this occasion?

In the middle of one of Malcolm's rare despondent moods Will Barker paid him a visit. He had a habit of turning up at the right time and on this occasion he brought some good news. Will had spent the weekend speaking to young people in the Midlands, in Nuneaton, at a Christian community called Lindley Lodge. It was an exciting place made up of a varied age group of people whose common link was their faith. Each one gave willingly of their time and skills with view to providing a place for young people to come and discover something of their own personalities and gifts. The warden of this community, the Reverend John Moore, was willing to consider Malcolm for a place working with the community on the estate team. It would provide him with

accommodation, food, work and the chance to live
with a group of Christian people who were all
committed to serving God in their lives.

Malcolm could hardly believe his ears. It was
everything he needed, everything he had feared
he would never get. He couldn't wait to tell Max
all about it and ask him to pray that God would
lead and guide him on this decision. Every part of
him wanted to say 'yes' right away, but he knew
this was an opportunity that he couldn't afford
to blunder into. He had to take time to think,
pray and consider all that it involved. Part of
that process involved a visit to the Midlands.

Within a few weeks Malcolm found himself
travelling alone on public transport from Haverigg
to Winson Green Prison in Birmingham, where
he stayed overnight in order to meet John Moore
and the rest of the community. It was the 21st
birthday of one of the girls. Malcolm thrived
on the happy and relaxed atmosphere as he
mingled with the community. All of them were
disappointed when the prison wouldn't grant
him permission to stay for the evening party.
Nevertheless, the outcome was positive, the start
of his new life on the outside of prison—never, he
thought, to return again.

In his last letter from Haverigg he records:

I am safely back from Lindley Lodge and
pleased to say I have been accepted by the
community there. What a wonderful set of
young people they are. I was put at ease as soon
as I arrived and made to feel really welcome.
What I did notice was that they accepted me

as a Christian and not as an ex-con. This has never happened before, possibly because I have never met anyone apart from in my prison uniform. It was absolutely marvellous, and I am looking forward to going on the 21st of next month [October]. I am sure that all that has happened to me since last September has been under the loving guidance of God's hand. How else can I explain it? I don't pretend to know very much about how or why God does what he does, but I do know with a cast-iron certainty that since being introduced to Jesus Christ my whole attitude to life has changed.

This will probably be my last letter to you from here. There is a certain custom in prison that anyone going out leaves a 'dropsy' to the lads who have been close to him. I will be buying 20 or 30 cigarettes to hand round next week, so I will not be buying any more letters. Anyway I shall try harder and harder for a closer fellowship with God in these last few weeks. Thank you for showing me how to become a Christian, Max. It seems such a long time since I was asking to see you in the police cells in Bradford. So much has changed for me since then. It is with much joy that I look forward to seeing you and Will on the twenty-first. Thank you for all your prayers, and your letters, without which—who knows? Every blessing, Malcolm

On October 21st 1971 at 6.30 am Malcolm Worsley was released from Haverigg Prison at the end of his seventh and last sentence. Waiting to greet him and drive him down to Lindley Lodge in the Midlands were his two most treasured friends and brothers in Christ: Will Barker and Max Wigley. Joe Isaacs, the Anglican prison chaplain, invited them all to breakfast before they set off on their journey. He greeted Malcolm warmly at the vicarage door with, 'Welcome, Malcolm. Call me Joe now.'

Seven

Lindley Lodge

Lindley Lodge in Nuneaton, Warwickshire, first opened as a Christian community and conference centre in 1970. In recent years the large house and estate has been sold to a Christian youth organisation called Youth With A Mission (YWAM). The specialist work of Lindley Lodge now continues at two other centres bearing the same name, one in Masham, North Yorkshire, and the other in Sheffield, South Yorkshire. The commitment to community life at all of the Lindley Lodge centres is of great importance and an integral part of the philosophy of life that it tries to convey to its visitors.

The mixed group of people living and working in the large house and grounds on the outskirts of Nuneaton in the seventies took that responsibility seriously. They aimed to provide a safe, secure and happy environment where young people could come and explore something of their personal attitudes towards work, leisure and the community in which they lived. Some members of the resident community offered their domestic skills, working on the teams responsible for the day-to-day running of the centre. Others worked in administration or on the estate buildings, while a number of others were employed specifically for their teaching and group work expertise—used in planning and leading the various courses. Their gender, marital status, age and experience of life varied, but they all shared a common belief in the Christian way of living and sought to live that out in their work and leisure as members of the community.

Malcolm had been accepted as a member of the team responsible for looking after the twelve-acre estate, including a large house which at that time accommodated up to 75 guests. He was sent with the backing and prayers of Haverigg's chaplain who had grown to know and respect his faith during his ten-month stay. In a letter of commendation to Lindley Lodge's warden, John Moore he wrote:

As I look back on my four years as chaplain here, with many men coming and going, and often returning, Malcolm's Christian witness has been outstandingly strong and effective. He has been devout and regular in worship, helpful in discussion groups (his hunger to learn is insatiable), and he has a special gift for recruiting and persuading others on behalf of his Lord. I pray he will be able to deal with temptations which will now come, but I am confident that he is capable of good work at counselling and encouraging others.

Will Barker was loved and respected by the

community at Lindley Lodge and his confidence in Malcolm had been a great influence in their decision to receive him into the community. John Moore prepared everyone as much as he felt able and right to do. The weekend visit had gone well and left little doubt in any of their minds as to the sincerity and determination of this man to make a new life for himself. They were united in the decision and prayerfully committed themselves to supporting and encouraging the newest member of their community.

Nobody was more aware of Malcolm's need of a family support at that time than Will Barker. He felt sure that God had provided in abundance for Malcolm in the community at Lindley Lodge but had no intention of withdrawing his own support. There would be times when he needed to get away from the larger community and be part of a smaller, more intimate family structure. Thus Will, his wife and children, all extended an open invitation to their home whenever Malcolm needed it. On off-duty days, weekends and holidays many of the community would go to be with their families, while Malcolm went to be with his own adopted family, the Barkers.

The arrival of Malcolm on 21st October 1971 remains vivid in the memories of the community who were there to greet him. Will Barker's familiar car with three men inside drew up outside the main entrance in the early afternoon. A small, pathetic-looking figure dressed in old, tattered clothes climbed out clutching two dirty paper carrier bags. There was no mistaking Malcolm. But as he lifted his head, there came a radiance from his eyes that was piercing; a gaze that expressed hope and eagerness. The smile that broke out across his scarred, pitted face relaxed them all. It was crystal clear to everyone that here was a man resolved to take every opportunity that this new life afforded him, and they felt privileged and delighted to be part of that process.

Community life became far more than a process to Malcolm. They became his family, a family lovingly given by God in which he could grow and flourish. Malcolm knew that he had so much to learn and wanted to go back to the very beginning and start life again as a child of God. Just as in any ordinary human family receiving a new baby there were adjustments to make, a lot of giving and taking, loving and forgiving. But there were also rewards and benefits for everyone.

All who knew Malcolm grew to love him and embraced him in the family of Lindley Lodge. Each had a part to play in the rebuilding and restoring of his new life, and their collective influence was to become the foundation upon which he would base the rest of his life. He eagerly studied each member and sought to imitate and adopt the Christlike qualities that he saw. He was never frightened to ask questions, invite criticism, or challenge his teachers should he think them wrong. In their grace and love they gently led and guided, careful never to push for fear of crushing this child of Christ in a man's body.

There was an understandable nervousness among the community in the early days, despite the fact they had done everything possible to welcome him. Pat had lovingly placed fresh flowers in his room, a gesture so small to her but gigantic in his eyes. No one had ever given him flowers before, and they became the start and a symbol of Pat's inner beauty and friendship, which he would always treasure. 'I've got a lot of bubbles of happiness inside me Malcolm,' she would say, 'and God wants me to share them with you.' Malcolm and Pat became brother and sister right from the beginning. Others were quick to follow.

The paper carrier bags he was holding on arrival contained all his worldly possessions: a Bible, a few letters and documents, a comb, toothbrush and razor. Having lived in prison uniform for so long, he had no clothes. Immediately the men gathered together a few outer garments to tide him over until he earned enough money to buy new ones. Malcolm was overwhelmed by their kindness, deeply moved and grateful for their generosity—but it was the package that lay on his bed on the second day of his stay that caused him to cry.

Placed neatly on his bed were two pairs of new underpants bought and given to him by a fellow member of the estate team. Merv was a joiner with the most brilliant sense of humour and sensitivity. Malcolm hadn't owned any underwear in years, and prison issue were never comfortable. On the outside he'd simply got used to wearing none. The fact that this man had bothered to think or notice this brought tears to his eyes. Receiving this gift was one of the most humbling moments of his life, and he felt

flooded with immense gratitude. Merv became
one of Malcolm's closest friends. They spent
long hours working together on the estate and
were never short of conversation or humour. It
was with people like Merv that Malcolm found
the confidence to talk and even laugh about his
own problems. Once, when deeply engrossed in
serious conversation about alcoholism, Malcolm
looked mischievously at Merv and said, with a
twinkle in his eye, 'You see Merv, I had to make
a choice between working, or drinking full time;
and work seemed to rather get in the way.' There
was always a funny side to life for Malcolm, and
Merv had a habit of bringing it out in him!

Ian couldn't have come from a more opposite
background and life style. He had left a pros-
perous job and luxurious home to serve on the
community of Lindley Lodge. Every advantage
and opportunity that life could offer had probably
come his way. And yet it was his humility and
self-discipline that Malcolm admired. He looked
up to him and tried earnestly to imitate the
determination and effort he put into Christian
discipleship. Ian never stopped working at his
faith and, as a direct result of his influence,
neither did Malcolm.

Bob became Malcolm's rock. He saw him as
Peter the Apostle—solid, dependable, always
there and willing to give of himself and his time.
As head of the estate team, Bob had immediate
responsibility for Malcolm, supervising and over-
seeing all his work. The community welcomed the
tradesman skills he brought with him, and he
became an invaluable resource to them. Not only

was he a highly skilled plasterer and bricklayer, but he developed the skills of an instructor always displaying tremendous patience with his new pupils. It was a joy and delight for Malcolm to be able to give something to others in this very practical way. He became a dedicated worker, and the community valued him and his skills enormously.

At first the risk of Malcolm returning to drinking was never far from the minds of the community. Following supper some weeks after his arrival Bob noticed he had disappeared. Feeling confident that he was either working on the estate or taking an early night, Bob joined a group who went off to the local pub for a drink. As they walked through the door, much to their dismay, sitting on a stool at the bar clutching a pint glass was Malcolm. Their hearts sank as they all looked towards him to handle the difficult moment. On closer examination Bob noticed that Malcolm's other hand was holding something else—his open Bible. And the glass contained a pint of Coke. Malcolm had grown impatient with the after-supper chatter, taken himself off to the local church, introduced himself to the vicar and decided to search out the local drunks for a spot of witnessing. He failed to understand the concern or anxiety on the faces of his new family! For them it was a tremendous relief to know that he would be able to take part in the very important social times with the young people in the local pubs without worrying if he would yield to the temptation to drink.

There were however anxious and difficult times

ahead. Prison had removed the sight and smell
of alcohol and the temptation with it. But every
prison sentence had done that, and Malcolm had
still returned to heavy drinking soon after each
release. Determined as he was on this occasion to
stay dry, it didn't automatically relieve his body
of the longing for alcohol. The overwhelming urge
came to the surface on a number of occasions,
and he knew that he had to learn to handle it.
It was at times like this that he desperately
needed the understanding and patience of his
new family. John Moore was among the first to
see him through one of these difficult periods soon
after his arrival. That particular night Malcolm
was wrestling with himself as every part of him
craved a drink. He knew that if he remained alone
he would lose the battle and so knocked on John
and Eileen's front door. Once inside he talked and
talked and John listened. When he could talk no
more they played table tennis and cards well into
the early hours of the morning. Only when John
was sure that he had worked through the crisis
did he allow him to return to his empty room and
be alone. Once there Malcolm turned to his Bible
for strength and consolation reading the words,
'I have the strength to face all conditions by the
power that Christ gives me.' They were written
by his hero Paul who had suffered unbearable
beatings and prison sentences for his faith.
Holding on to that promise he felt sure that
he was going to overcome the alcohol struggle.

Never a day passed when Malcolm wasn't
learning new skills for living. Simply waking,
dressing, working, talking, eating and playing

with others were all major challanges in his life. He threw himself head first into everything and anything he could, barely stopping for a moment in case he missed an opportunity. Sleeping always seemed such waste of time! His enthusiasm once gave him a broken leg during a football game and weeks of misery for the community as they discovered that he was a terrible patient. A pot-legged Malcolm became a comical sight as he hobbled around the estate, determined to keep working. But it was his dress sense that drew the attention of most guests. In direct contrast to the dull grey prison uniform, as soon as his wages allowed him, he bought the brightest and gaudiest coloured clothes he could find. Colour co-ordination was not among his gifts. Many felt he was reflecting his inner happiness on the outside in a very graphic way, while others thought he ought to tone it down a bit!

As the months went by, Malcolm became desperate to work out the right way to live, to find a lifestyle and philosophy that was totally Christian, that would guarantee him 'success' in the ways of God. His first model had been St Paul and now he had John, Eileen, Pat, Bob, Ian, Merv, Sue and others. But they were all different; some single, some married, from varying backgrounds, Christian traditions and spiritualities. He fought for a clear definition and structure, longing to be the same as those he loved and admired. If only everything could be clear, black and white—but it wasn't. Shirley presented him with his greatest problem so far. She was a wealthy lady. Malcolm decided he had to tell her that it was wrong

to be rich as a Christian and that she had no
right to own thousands of pounds when there
were people hungry and homeless in the world.
Shirley invited him to supper one evening in her
flat to discuss the problem.

The problem of money was easily resolved in
Malcolm's eyes. 'You should just give it all away,'
he blatantly informed Shirley. She listened gra-
ciously as he off-loaded all his bitterness and
resentment towards all who were anything but
working-class or poor. He pronounced judgement
on any Christian who dare store more than a
week's wages or own anything other than life's
bare essentials. He knew what it was like, how
little one needed to live off, and he would show
them how to manage. In fact, at that time,
Malcolm thought he had the answers to most
problems.

When he had finished his speech, in her own
quiet, gentle and loving way, Shirley asked
where he might have been now if it hadn't
been for Lindley Lodge. He admitted that he
wasn't sure what would have happened to him.
She pointed out that places like this demanded
capital investment and asked him how he would
decide between the kind of investment where
the 'results' would perhaps be unknown, or
in feeding a few hundred hungry people in
the world. He went very quiet. She asked him
whether he would give thousands of pounds away
in one fell swoop or invest so that the money
would make more money to give over a longer
period of time. Malcolm lowered his head. Shirley
asked him if he would like the responsibility of

deciding, when hundreds of needs became known
to her, which needy cause she should give to and
which to turn down. Malcolm's silence said it
all. Shirley offered him the responsibility that
accompanied wealth, and he shied away feeling
inadequate and daunted.

Malcolm came away indebted to Shirley for yet
another important lesson in life. He had taken
one more step along the road towards understanding that everyone's circumstances were different and all are called to be a good steward of
what God has given them. He had no right to
judge anyone else and was learning to appreciate that no two people were the same. He
was also discovering that he was an individual,
unique in personality and gifting and it was all
God-given. He had to learn what was right
for himself, not only in the area of steward-
ship but the whole shape and direction of his
life's work. That life work began at Lindley
Lodge.

The evening in the pub was the start of regular
visits to Nuneaton town although not always to
the same place. Clutching his tattered New Testament, Malcolm walked the streets and parks
searching out the homeless. He knew where
to find them, how they felt, spoke a language
that they understood and loved them dearly.
The gospel that Malcolm proclaimed was for
the lost, lonely and homeless, and it spoke to
their bodies, minds and spirits. He talked to the
unlovely, wept with those who hurt, befriended
those whom society had rejected and where possible fed the hungry. Some he even brought home

with him to the Lodge, expecting others to accommodate their many needs as he did. He had no idea of the problems he created and the disruption to community life! Sensitively and with concern not to squash the growing concern Malcolm was so obviously developing for the homeless, the community gently reminded him of the main ministry of Lindley Lodge and his job within it. Eager as he always was to learn, he understood and accepted the position, agreeing to restrict his male visitors to his own room and females to the room of any girl in the community who was willing to take them. And all of this had to be in his own time.

Maureen was one of the first young girls he tried to help. Rumour had it that she was living rough and sleeping among the bushes in the local park. No one could persuade her to come out. The nights were getting dark and cold, and there was tremendous concern for her health and well-being. Accompanied by one of the girls from the Lodge, Malcolm sat on a park bench talking in a loud voice, 'I know you're there Maureen. I don't want to hurt you, just help you. Why not come out and have some soup that I've brought for you.' There was no response. After several attempts he left the flask on the bench, telling her to help herself and he would come back later. It worked, and the pattern continued for several nights. Maureen would drink the soup, eat some sandwiches and return the empty flask for Malcolm to collect later. This long-drawn-out process paid off eventually, as her confidence grew until she felt able to trust Malcolm sufficiently to face him. A very scared, dirty and hungry young girl appeared from the bushes. She was scantily dressed with a face plastered in black mascara. There was little doubt that she would not have survived many more days and nights in those conditions. Maureen was the first of many to be on the receiving end of the love and hope expressed in Malcolm. She accompanied them back to Lindley Lodge, where she shared a single room with one of the secretaries for three to four months.

Such caring was a natural and spontaneous part of his being and part of the new Malcolm who was emerging from within Lindley Lodge. His personal growth and new understanding of life was refreshing and challenging to everyone who worked with him. He became a much-loved and valued member of the community, working not only on the estate team but later as a group leader and tutor on the courses. The transition from the estate to the training side was gradual. At first he would accompany small groups on outdoor activities, giving support and encouragement in an informal atmosphere. But it quickly became clear that Malcolm had an understanding and empathy with the young people that could be used in other areas too. His skill in relating to the youngsters was invaluable, and in time he became a much appreciated tutor.

While the primary aim of Lindley Lodge was not evangelism, the Christian way of life and prayer foundation laid down by members of the community gave rise to many opportunities for

faith sharing. Malcolm took every opportunity he
could. The place was unimportant—a pub, the
coffee bar, disco dance floor or simply walking
and talking. Somehow Malcolm found a way to
speak for his God. Sometimes his reputation
went before him, and one or two youngsters
anticipated the challenge with mixed emotions.
On one occasion a rather extrovert green-haired
young man made his feelings quite clear. 'You're
not going to tell me about Jesus, are you?' he
challenged Malcolm.

'Not unless you want me to,' came the reply.
Nothing else was said about the subject for the
next four days until the youth suddenly declared,
'I know you're only waiting for an opportunity to
tell me about Jesus, so get on with it!' Malcolm
did. Some five or six days later, at the end of the
course, the group was enjoying the final disco
when the same young man approached Malcolm
on the dance floor. He seemed unaware of the
booming record blaring out of the speakers as
he spoke to Malcolm. 'I've just been upstairs
in your chapel—I've never known so much love
from people before—I want your Jesus!' Unable
to wait until the record was finished or find a
suitable, quiet place to talk, he dropped to his
knees on the dance floor and asked Malcolm
to pray with him. It was Malcolm's joy and
privilege to do so.

Life was full at Lindley Lodge, and Malcolm
loved every minute of it. In between working
and witnessing he still found time to spend in
Nuneaton working on the streets and in the pubs,
his desire to reach the homeless now increasing

by the day. Members of the community encouraged him, and some accompanied him, eager to learn from Malcolm's expertise. One of his most frequent companions was the secretary who had so willingly shared her room with Maureen. She was called Jennifer.

Eight

Jennifer

Jennifer Spensley grew up in some of Cumbria's most beautiful countryside. The small country town of Appleby was an idyllic setting with a strong, stable community life in which children and young people thrived. Their world was tranquil and privileged, rarely touched by the troubles and traumas of the outside world. The Spensley family was respectable and hardworking and well thought of by the local people. The behaviour of the children both inside and outside the home mattered a lot to their parents, and great emphasis was placed upon good behaviour and impeccable manners. Appearances mattered in a close-knit community like Appleby, and the family strived at all times to maintain a good reputation.

As the years went by Mr and Mrs Spensley had good reason to be proud of their children, with one son at Cambridge, a daughter at London University, and Jennifer—while not so obviously academic—clearly making a career for herself, first as a legal secretary, and later as a teacher. Harold, the youngest child, was born mentally

handicapped, unable to speak. The family, especially Jennifer who stayed at home longer than
her brother and sister, were devoted to caring
for him. It was a close-knit and secure family
for Jennifer.

As church warden Mr Spensley ensured that
his children had a Church of England upbringing.
Both Jennifer and her younger sister Rachel
attended church regularly each Sunday and
were familiar with basic Christian teachings
and church festivals. But their commitment to
church and God was more out of respect and
obedience to their parents than religious fervour
or spiritual hunger. It wasn't until the physics
teacher at school invited them to mid-week Bible
studies that they realised that there was any
more to Christianity than sitting through a
weekly service.

At first attending the group was a novelty, one of
the rare 'social' outings that their strict upbringing allowed and therefore not to be missed! But
as time went on they began to learn about and
understand the Bible in a way that they had
never been taught in all their days of church
going. The Christian life was explained to them
as a relationship with a person rather than a
set of rules and code of behaviour. It demanded
a response from them. The Bible studies then
led them on to young people's camps, where
they joined others in the exciting discovery of
a personal relationship with Jesus. As teenagers
both Rachel and Jennifer committed their lives to
God, promising to seek his guidance and leading
at every important stage of their lives.

It was a clear call from God over ten years later that brought Jennifer to Lindley Lodge. Following some years working in Edinburgh, training to teach in Huddersfield and a teaching post in Desford, Leicester, she was invited by John Moore to join the community as his secretary. It was a costly decision, but there was no doubt in Jennifer's mind that this was the right one. The sacrifice of a secure career, a teacher's salary, and the freedom and privacy of her own home and life paled into insignificance in the light of God's new direction for her work and life at Lindley Lodge.

Her parents were mystified by their daughter's change of direction, but Rachel, who had shared digs with Jennifer in Leicester, supported and encouraged her in her decision, firmly believing God had called her to work there. They spent a happy Christmas together as a family in Appleby before Jennifer moved out ready to start work in January.

Malcolm had been part of the community for just three months. Jennifer's immediate attraction towards him as a person was not unusual. His warmth, sincerity and magnetic personality had attracted community and guests alike. Still unsure of what might be 'acceptable' social skills, Malcolm had decided it was far easier to display his loving heart to all he met, regardless of who they were or what the occasion might be. Consequently many lives were automatically drawn towards him. Jennifer was no exception.

His dramatic testimony to the power of God in

his life left this quiet country girl quite speechless. She'd never heard anything like it. He was the living miracle that she'd always been sure God could perform, the sort of experience she'd read about in Christian books but never met first-hand before now. She listened to his every word and became fascinated by his tales. He was so honest and sincere about his faith. His commitment to God was one hundred per cent and his life totally dedicated to the task of telling others about Jesus. That in itself was appealing to her. Jennifer found that she could talk to him quite openly and freely about many different things without embarrassment. He made her feel safe and secure and became a real rock on whom she learned to rest and depend in times of need. She was a highly gifted and able person in her own right, yet in this man she saw qualities and resources that she loved and valued. And more important than anything else, he had the most brilliant sense of humour! Malcolm never lost an opportunity to joke or tease and frequently provoked endless times of laughter through his own infectious giggle. Their friendship blossomed in this lovely environment of work, play and prayer.

What emerged in time as a two-way attraction did not go unnoticed. Community members and guests often commented on the quality of their working relationship and friendship. The intensity of community life, working, living and socialising together meant that personal relationships often developed very quickly. Jennifer had not realised just how quickly and deeply Malcolm's

affection for her had grown until just a few
months after her arrival he appeared in her office
one day with a attractively wrapped present.

The watch was beautiful: small, delicate and
very feminine. It had cost him all he had managed to save since arriving at Lindley Lodge.
This overwhelming expression of affection from
Malcolm spoke volumes and caused Jennifer to
think seriously about her own feelings towards
him. At that time she felt unable to return the
same degree of affection openly but was very
concerned not to cause him any hurt or sense
of rejection. She knew that the watch had cost
him far more than just money. In the giving of
that gift Malcolm had given part of himself.

It would have been difficult to distance herself
from him in the community, and Jennifer had
no desire to do that, though she realised it
was important that their time together became
increasingly work-based, with less time spent
alone socially. Working with Malcolm in the
evenings provided the ideal opportunity for this.
More often than anyone else in the community,
she joined him night after night walking the
streets of Nuneaton searching out the homeless
and needy. If her love for him was to grow, she
was confident that it would find the necessary
time and space in their work together.

There was so much to learn from this man.
She didn't want to miss a thing. Her sheltered
upbringing had protected her from any knowledge, let alone sight, of the homeless, alcoholics
and prostitutes. She envied Malcolm's understanding, his ability to communicate and the

deep compassion he had in his heart for them. At
first she watched carefully, learning about their
sad conditions, but as time went on she became
deeply involved and committed to helping many.
They came to trust her and depend upon the
friendship and acceptance that she offered alongside Malcolm. They made an excellent team,
each needing the other as they worked with
both men and women. Their commitment to
the work and to one another increased by the
day, reaching the stage a few months later when
Jennifer welcomed an invitation to spend a day
out together in the Lake District. No doubt the
Lake District has been the backdrop for many
a romance and proposal of marriage with its
vast expanses of lakeland water and aspiring
hills. But it wasn't Malcolm's choice of scenery
on this particular day. The all-too-familiar view
of Haverigg prison became the background for
their leisurely walk. As they wandered hand
in hand along the beach overlooking the dunes
and daunting prison complex, Malcolm invited
Jennifer to accept his invitation of marriage.
Without hesitation, she said yes.

She was twenty-eight years old and very much
in love. Even with the prison building dominating
the scene, thoughts of Malcolm's past were far
from her mind. Jennifer's eyes looked only to
the future. Beyond Lindley Lodge that future
was unknown, but the strength and security
this couple found in each other and in God
gave them confidence and courage to look ahead.
Being married to Malcolm, she thought, her
future was forced to be different—a challenge, a

journey of faith and adventure. That sunny July
afternoon became the start of an adventure that
would bring them back to the small Cumbrian
town of Haverigg more times than they could
ever imagine.

After choosing a small and inexpensive ring
(priceless to them) from a local jeweller's shop,
Jennifer and Malcolm drove the short distance to
her parents' home in Appleby. Naturally nervous
of their response, Malcolm was eager to do everything correctly and in order and so decided to ask
Mr Spensley formally for his daughter's hand
in marriage. While Jennifer had spoken to her
parents about Malcolm's wonderful testimony,
they did not fully appreciate the details of his
past. They saw no advantage in hiding the facts
and so decided that Malcolm should tell them
everything.

Sensing an air of importance about the visit,
Mr Spensley invited Malcolm into the front room,
leaving Jennifer and her mother alone together
in the living-room. Malcolm began his tale looking carefully for indications of approval or disapproval. Neither was forthcoming. On the surface
Mr Spensley seemed to be receiving it all without
difficulty, but Malcolm knew that it was a lot
for any devoted father to take on board in one
hearing. Wherever possible he tried to emphasise
the future, his commitment to Jennifer and their
desire to serve God together. He spoke for some
time without being interrupted. However, Mr
Spensley continued to listen, nodding occasionally but saying nothing.

Malcolm was left feeling confused and unsure

of what reaction he was getting, hoping for the best but fearing the worst. The bemused couple left the family home a short time later feeling they had done all they could but knowing that while disapproval had not been openly expressed neither had the slightest hint of approval been given. As they drove down the motorway they suspected that heated words were being exchanged in the household at that very moment. Only time would tell.

Having decided not to allow the limited response of her parents to dampen their special day, they drove enthusiastically back to Lindley Lodge to share their happy news. The reaction couldn't have been more different. Shrieks of delight, hugs and kisses, and celebrations went on all around the house. Few were surprised and everyone was overjoyed for the happy couple.

The bubble of happiness in Malcolm's and Jennifer's lives burst quite suddenly only a few days later. Arriving by first-class delivery came a carefully constructed letter from her parents. The contents were bold, leaving no doubt whatsoever as to their feelings and intentions concerning the proposed marriage. As far as they were concerned, it was quite out of the question; and they intended to enlist the support of as many senior people they could, including the Bishop of Coventry, to ensure that the marriage didn't take place. Letters to these people had already been sent.

The letter fulfilled their worst fears and stunned them into silence. Slowly the tears began to fall, not out of anger or bitterness, but out of a deep

sense of sorrow and compassion for two loving
and protective parents. They understood their
fears, some of which were shared by others.
Malcolm's own mother had cautiously reminded
Jennifer of the hurt and pain he'd caused his
first wife and sons. Jennifer was not blind to
the difficulties she knew she would face living
with a man bearing the scars of an alcoholic,
still a heavy smoker, and living with the ghost
of a criminal record. They were real problems,
and she knew they wouldn't go overnight, but
God had promised, 'I will never leave you, I will
never abandon you!', and that was a promise she
knew would carry her through. What she hadn't
been prepared for and could well live without was
this direct opposition from her family at the start.
Malcolm was a new creation, and she longed for
them to see him in that light.

Despite letters and visits from Jennifer and
other supportive people attempting to play go-
between there was no changing her parents'
minds. Attempts on their part to enlist the
support of senior officials in the church had
failed. Eventually the wedding date was fixed
for Sunday September 24th at Kirby Muxlow
Baptist church.

There was no shortage of enthusiasm and
helpers. Preparations for the day became the joy
and delight of the entire community. Planning
the catering, transport, photography, flower arr-
anging, cake decorating, music, and finding a
best man, sidesmen and bridesmaid involved
just about every individual at Lindley Lodge.
The wedding dress was made by Malcolm's old

Sunday school teacher from childhood days in
Preston who, delighted to know of his faith
and transformation, wanted also to contribute
towards the special day. Will Barker, Malcolm's
faithful prison visitor and friend, was given the
greatest honour of all—to give the bride away.
He had been more than a father to this couple
and shared fully in their joy and delight on this
tremendous occasion. Jennifer's family support
at the service came from a few aunts and her
sister Rachel, who had married earlier that summer. She stood by Jennifer, in every respect, as
her matron of honour.

Over a hundred guests crowded into the small
chapel that Sunday afternoon. It was harvest
festival weekend, and the whole building was
decorated with fruits, flowers and vegetables—a
beautiful sight. The ceremony was bound to be
different simply by its circumstances, but there
was no doubt in anyone's mind just how different
it was going to be when the Bridal March struck
up on the organ. As Jennifer appeared at the top
of the aisle, arm linked to Will, the impatient
groom decided he was going to meet his bride
half way. Turning in full view of the congreation
Malcolm walked swiftly down the aisle taking
Jennifer by the hand and leading her back to
the front of the church. There wasn't a dry eye
in the church.

Accompanied by a community member on the
guitar the congregation stood to sing 'Amazing
Grace! How sweet the sound that saved a wretch
like me. I once was lost but now am found.
Was blind but now I see.' God's grace abounded

that day as two very special people were joined
together in marriage by God.

The newlyweds' first home was a small flat
within the estate reserved for married couples
serving the community. During the day their
work continued on the team and in the office, and
where possible the evenings were spent working together on the streets of Nuneaton. Being
married gave Malcolm and Jennifer additional
freedom in helping the homeless. Their increased
joint income and flat enabled them to offer practical help in terms of clothing, food, warmth and
shelter. Very soon they were accommodating a
homeless man and woman, Bob and Maureen.
There was no extended honeymoon. Life was
full and busy, but everything that they had ever
wanted. The discovery, rather more quickly than
expected, that Jennifer was pregnant, added to
their joy. The honeymoon baby was expected in
June 1973.

There was only one name both of them wanted
for their firstborn, namely Paul after St Paul,
the life of whom had influenced Malcolm only
two years earlier. His arrival was surrounded
with joy and happiness not least because of the
reconciliation that the pregnancy had brought
between the Worsleys and the Spensleys. While
Jennifer had continued to write regularly since
the wedding, informing her parents of all that
was happening in their lives, it was the news
that they were about to become grandparents
that had softened their hearts. Seeds of healing
and reconciliation were sown and grew steadily
as the years passed. (During Mr Spensley's very

serious illness nearly twenty years later he asked
to speak with Malcolm alone. The two were more
than father and son-in-law; they had become
friends and soulmates. He died just a few months
later.)

The Worsley household now totalled five.
Jennifer endeavoured to feed, clothe and accommodate them all, fitting in additional duties in
the community wherever possible. Transformed
from an alcoholic to a workaholic, Malcolm packed
in as many hours as he could on the streets and
in the pubs. Their deep concern for the homeless
increased by the day.

Local churches in Nuneaton were well aware
of the presence of Lindley Lodge and welcomed
the opportunities for ecumenical contact that it
offered them. Malcolm was especially keen to
build stronger links between the denominations,
uniting all Christians in the task of bringing the
gospel to the whole town. He made every effort to
inform and involve any who showed an interest
in his work on the streets and regularly spoke to
church groups about the work.

Part of his ecumenical involvement took both
him and Jennifer, just a few months after Paul
was born, to London to attend a national conference on evangelism. The well-known evangelist,
Dr Billy Graham, spoke powerfully of the need
for local churches to respond to the glaring conditions of the socially deprived in the country,
especially the homeless. At the end of the evening
he invited people to commit themselves publicly
to this work. Separated by thousands of people
across the vast auditorium in Earls Court, both

Jennifer and Malcolm stood to commit their lives to reaching the homeless and needy wherever and however God should lead them. It was only later that evening that each told the other of their response. Paul, just three months old and fast asleep in his push-chair, was also to become an integral part of that family ministry.

As they journeyed home to the Midlands at the end of the week, they knew that the last few days had become a turning point in their lives and ministries. What the future held they didn't know, but the one thing they both felt sure of was that the time had come, however painful it might be, to break away from their family at Lindley Lodge.

Nine

St James, Weddington

Guy Cornwall-Jones had been the rector of St James, Weddington, since 1964. While he was studying English at Cambridge he came to a personal faith in Christ during a university mission. This was the first of many led by a London-based clergyman called John Stott. Thus after Cambridge Guy offered himself for ordination training and soon returned to college to study theology.

St James was his first church and his first opportunity to put into practice all he had learned. A small but determined nucleus of people made up the congregation, but the first seven years were an uphill struggle. Lindley Lodge was on the parish boundary and so a 'two-way street' between Guy and the community naturally developed. Guy received encouragement and fellowship there, and individual members of the community joined the worshipping congregation of St James.

The first of these was David, a mechanic in his early twenties, who had met the Holy Spirit in a powerful way. Through prayer and Bible reading

he brought a special ministry of prophecy and
encouragement to the church family. At the
same time Guy was also helped by a travelling
preacher from the Plymouth Brethren church
called Peter Brandon. Through Peter's teaching
ministry, he came to a deeper understanding of
the work of the Cross in his own life—one that
had a powerful impact on his ministry. God was
preparing him individually and the St James
people corporately for an important time ahead.

It was nearly two years later in January 1973,
a few months after marrying Jennifer, that
Malcolm first had clear guidance from God to
join St James, Weddington. 'God has sent me to
join your church,' he told the tall, refined English
vicar as he stood on the vicarage doorstep. Of
course it wasn't the first time Malcolm had made
bold declarations on vicarage doorsteps but, at
least, on this occasion, he wasn't quite such a
risk! Guy responded politely by inviting him in
and went on to share with him all that God had
been saying to them as a church in the last two
or three years. Malcolm identified strongly with
part of the prophetic word they were hearing and
felt sure he had a very specific part to play in the
life of this church family. Then in his own turn
he shared with Guy his own vision for reaching
people in body, mind and spirit, especially the
homeless. All his concerns were very close to the
things that God had laid on Guy's heart.

As the weeks and months progressed Guy
became Malcolm's confident, listening carefully
to many of his present frustrations. He felt
called to be his Barnabas, introducing him to

the other apostles, encouraging and releasing
his friend into a wider ministry. He wondered
if Malcolm ought to have more training from
others with greater experience of working with
the homeless. With this in mind, he arranged
a trip to St George's church in Leeds, where
he knew there was an extensive ministry going
on among the 'down and outs' in the city. This
would provide an opportunity for Malcolm to
see a different situation and allow him to test
his calling for the work in Nuneaton. During
the journey the two men relaxed and chatted
about a number of things, not least their vision
for the future. On their way home they stopped
at a service station and Guy drew Malcolm's
attention twowards a smart Jaguar. As they
stood admiring the car's sleek lines, they commented on the unusual licence plate—ACT 132B.
Guy smiled and suggested light-heartedly that
it could be a Bible reference. Opening his New
Testament in the car, Malcolm turned to the Acts
of the Apostles, 13:2, and read the second half of
the verse 'Set apart for me Barnabas and Paul for
the work to which I have called them'. There was
now no doubt in Guy's mind that he and Malcolm
were to work together and that they were in the
right place.

Malcolm and Guy met regularly to pray together
on Saturdays at 6 am. It was during this
time that they developed a vision for a united
church work in Nuneaton. Even in his prison
days Malcolm had never seen much point in
denominations and worked tirelessly, if with
little success, to unite the different services there.

In Nuneaton there were thriving congregations of Baptists, Weslyan Reform, Roman Catholics, Anglicans, URC, Pentecostals, Methodists and Plymouth Brethren. The two men felt sure that if these people could be united in their vision for the proclamation of the gospel message in Nuneaton, God would do wonderful things.

With this vision Guy and Malcolm invited church leaders from all the denominations to meet at Lindley Lodge. An open, warm spirit of sharing emerged, during which time the Plymouth Brethren told of their plans for an Easter mission in 1974. The preacher invited was Peter Brandon, who had been such a help and encouragement to Guy only a few years earlier. As these leaders talked, prayed and waited on God a clearer vision emerged for a united town wide mission, and the Brethren offered their plans as a basis for it. The decision was unanimous; prayer and planning began immediately. Quite independently, the Bishop of Coventry, Dr Cuthbert Bardsley, announced his decision to send a four-person team of Church Army evangelists to Nuneaton from September 1973. They soon became an integral part of the mission, and Malcolm emerged as one of several gifted evangelists in the group, as well as an important link between different denominations.

Malcolm was inspired by all these developments but also frustrated. He wanted to devote more and more time to working with the homeless and using his evangelistic gifts locally in the churches. Guy had already welcomed him into the pulpit of St James, where he had shared his

testimony and preached the gospel. His study
in prison had given him some excellent Bible
qualifications which went a long way towards
his being considered as a Church of England lay
reader. Because of his exceptional background
and growing ministry in the diocese, the bishop
invited Malcolm to talk with him. A half-hour
interview was sandwiched between two other
important engagements, so he was quite tired
when Malcolm arrived. Fortunately all he had to
do on this occasion was listen as Malcolm poured
forth the tale of how he had become a Christian
and all that God had done in his life since.
Cuthbert Bardsley was enthralled and, forgetting
his next appointment, encouraged Malcolm to
continue his story. After an hour he finally rose
to his feet saying, 'What a delight, I must give
you a blessing, Malcolm.' He raised his hands
and rested them on Malcolm's head. 'May God
bless you, Malcolm,' he said. Totally unaware of
Anglican ceremony, Malcolm placed his hands on
the bishop's head, also saying, 'And God bless you
too, bishop.' A delighted Cuthbert Bardsley flung
open the doors to his study declaring to his next
visitor, 'How wonderful, I've just been blessed.
Bishops need blessings too. How wonderful!' The
two men were to meet on many occasions in the
future and always delighted in remembering the
day the bishop received a blessing.

In the midst of the excitement, the changes
locally and his search for an answer to present
frustrations, Malcolm put a suggestion to Guy.
'Perhaps we should just leave Lindley Lodge and
live by faith continuing the work that way?' he

said. Guy was cautious in his reply but hinted it might well be a possibility and rather casually admitted that they had been considering sharing their home with other Christians. It was a passing comment, more thinking aloud than a serious offer. He was about to learn something very important about his friend 'Paul', that, given the slightest encouragement, he acted fast.

Only days later Malcolm stood once more on the vicarage doorstep saying, 'Jennifer and I have handed in our notice at Lindley Lodge. When can we move in? Oh, and you were including Maureen and Pat (the most recent additions to their household) in the invitation, weren't you?' Standing listening to Malcolm, Guy struggled to remember if he had even mentioned this passing comment to his wife Helen. Perhaps if he'd deliberated for too long the decision would never have been made, but this, he felt, was just a little too fast! In an attempt to slow down the process slightly the Cornwall-Jones and the Worsleys agreed to explore and pray through the possibility and practicability of the suggestion. After much deliberation, and to avoid any unreal expectations or false hopes, they finally decided upon a committment of three months, at the end of which time Malcolm and Jennifer agreed to find alternative accommodation.

By the end of November 1973 the five members of the Worsley household had moved into two rooms at Weddington Rectory. Only a few weeks later they discovered that the sixth member was well on its way; Jennifer was pregnant again, with Paul just five months old.

The urgency to find their own accommodation was increased by the impending birth of a second baby. Guy and Helen were marvellous in sharing their home, never allowing them to feel visitors but always members of this rapidly extending family. Their own first child, Ruth, was just under four years of age. The differing life styles took some adjusting to, especially where Maureen and Pat were concerned, but they coped without complaint or ill feeling.

Malcolm was never happier, dividing his time between helping Guy at St James and working on the streets, as well as doing everything that he could towards to the Easter mission. Jennifer was naturally tired with a young baby and a second due later that year. She took responsibility for the day-to-day organising of the two girls, encouraging them to share the workload where ever possible. They had no regular income of any kind, living completely by faith, but God never let them down. Many members of St James admired their courage and conviction and regularly provided clothing, gifts of food and sometimes money. Most of all they prayed for them. At other times gifts would appear on the doorstep and through the letter box with no indication of their senders. In Malcolm's and Jennifer's minds this provision confirmed that they were in the right place, doing what God had called them to do.

Their low earnings at Lindley Lodge hadn't given much of an opportunity to save, so looking for a house to buy seemed impossible. Malcolm approached the council about renting a property.

It wasn't ideal because of the continual coming
and going of homeless girls that they anticipated,
feeling sure that the council might object to their
property being used in this way. In the event they
were indeed refused a council house, but, much to
their surprise and delight, were offered instead
a 100% mortgage on a property they could buy.
It was a miracle! Not only did Malcolm have no
regular income with which to repay the mortgage but he could offer no financial guarantee
other than confidently telling the council God
would provide!

Duke Street was not in the most desirable area
in Nuneaton. Its old terraced houses were severely
neglected. Because properties were cheaper, many
of the Asian community had moved into the
district, resulting in a mass exodus of white
English occupants. The Worsleys were undisturbed by colour of skin, language or culture.
It might not be a palace or particularly fit for
human habitation (yet!), but the end terrace on
Duke Street was their first house, and they were
proud of it. Malcolm thanked God again for the
building skills he had acquired early in his life
and started on the long task of making the house
into a home.

For £1,200 they gained two bedrooms and a
bathroom upstairs, two living rooms and a minute
kitchen downstairs. The house might not have
seemed large to anyone else but to them it was
more than double the space they'd had before—and
therefore allowed for accommodation of double the
number of homeless. Together as they tore through
endless layers of wallpaper, all seemingly stuck

together with garlic and spices, Malcolm and
Jennifer decided how they would organise the
house. It made sense for them to occupy the two
rooms upstairs with Paul and the new baby, while
downstairs in one of the living rooms they would
place two sets of bunk beds to take up to four
homeless girls at any one time. The second living
room would double as a dining room, which would
no doubt be very crowded at times. The kitchen
was the biggest concern, and if Jennifer was going
to fit more than herself in it, an extension was
needed. The building would be no problem, but
finding the time in which to do it might prove
difficult. Jennifer knew that Malcolm needed a
deadline, so they decided it had to be complete
by the time Jennifer came out of hospital with
the new baby.

The biggest distraction to building and redecorating was the Easter mission. The United Reformed Church in Nuneaton seated 1,000 people
so naturally became the venue for the nightly
meetings. A hundred people came on the first
night and sat huddled together at the back of
the hall. The atmosphere was cold and stilted,
leaving the Christians discouraged and confused.
They'd been so sure that it was God's will to have
a united mission they couldn't understand why
the response was so poor. The planning group
met to pray the following morning. The outcome
was not what any of them had expected or
especially wanted, as God seemed to confront
them with their divisions and differences. It
was indeed a *united* mission he had wanted,
the denominations working together as the one

body of Christ. Instead disagreement, pride and deep-seated resentments had to be dealt with.

Malcolm decided to talk about an experience he had had a few weeks earlier. He explained how during the time he had been meeting to pray with a small number of church leaders he had begun to feel strangely on the outside of that group. However hard he tried to push himself into the circle, he remained on the edge. While wrestling in prayer over the matter, he received a clear image in his mind of a large bubble. The bubble was Christ, and within it his group of friends were praying. During the course of the day, as he continued to pray, the bubble slowly absorbed him, and God spoke powerfully about being 'in Christ'. Malcolm then came to a fresh understanding of what being 'in Christ' meant and how his own efforts to be part of the body of Christ had been in vain. Only as he focused on Jesus and submitted totally to him did he feel part of the group around him.

Peter Brandon, leader of the mission, took Malcolm's vision and applied it to what was happening now. He invited the people at the prayer meeting to stand and link hands with their friends around them and then asked if they thought that this was an expression of Christian unity. Nearly everyone did. Peter observed that the group was looking at each other and quietly suggested that real unity, as Malcolm had discovered, came in looking into Jesus. He asked them to turn inwards and look upwards, focusing on Christ but still linking hands. It became a

painful and yet powerful time of learning for
them all as God poured his Holy Spirit upon the
mission. Each night the numbers at the evening
meetings grew until, on the last evening, the hall
was packed.

The Christian church in Nuneaton and district
grew in numbers and strength. The months and
years that followed were a remarkable testimony
to renewal and revival with hundreds of individuals committing their lives to Christ and a
unity between denominations never previously
experienced. Malcolm continued to initiate and
lead many inter-denominational gatherings. St
James became a centre for renewal through
weekly ecumenical praise and worship meetings, sometimes inviting outside speakers and
on other occasions using local ministers. One of
the most memorable gatherings was the presentation of a popular Christian musical called
'Come Together', in the Baptist Church. Malcolm
himself preached to a packed congregation of
over a thousand people. His gifts were becoming
widely known and used by God. In recognition of
his vital part in renewal and evangelism Bishop
Cuthbert Bardsley gave him permission to act
as an evangelist within the diocese, giving him
a wider and more recognised ministry. In place
of his blue lay reader's scarf he now wore the
bright red scarf of an evangelist, with pride and
thankfulness.

With the mission over, kitchen extension completed and baby Helen safely delivered into the
world, Malcolm and Jennifer prepared to receive
their first new residents into Duke Street. Every

one of them came off the streets either through Malcolm's own contacts or by referral from individuals or groups who knew of their work. In later months the offical bodies of social and probation services began to seek out Malcolm and Jennifer to reach those whom they could not. Angie was one such, among the first to occupy one of the four bunks in Duke Street's downstairs bedroom. She was just seventeen years old, seven months pregnant, kicked out of home and found living in the back of an abandoned mini van. Malcolm went to try to persuade her to come and live with them. Angie was scared and lonely. She'd heard about 'the vicar' as the street folk of Nuneaton had nicknamed Malcolm but, desperate as she was, had no intention of getting preached at in her condition. Malcolm stood patiently reassuring her and willing her to step out of the van. There was never any active preaching or teaching in the home. Malcolm and Jennifer had decided they simply had to live out their faith, allowing their actions to do the speaking unless directly asked or invited to do otherwise by the girls. On this occasion his patience was rewarded as Angie agreed to accompany him home, where she stayed until her baby was born.

Wherever possible the girls continued in their jobs, contributing to the upkeep of the house when they could. But the majority were unemployed or, as in Carol's case, earned their living through prostitution. Keeping Carol occupied and off the streets wasn't easy. She had come from a wealthy middle-class family where she had been brought up in emotionally sterile conditions. Starved of physical affection and any demonstration of love from either parent, Carol discovered at thirteen that some people did want to touch her. What started as kissing and cuddling behind the bike shed at school had developed into full-scale prostitution by the time she was 15. She became obsessed, often going with five or six men a night, unable to control herself. She hated herself and the obsession that possessed her, often spending hours and hours helplessly crying in the arms of Jennifer or Malcolm. They were probably the only arms she had ever known to offer her unconditional love and acceptance.

There were many times in those early days at Duke Street when Malcolm risked life and limb to protect the girls. Angie came running home one day pleading for him to rescue another of the girls called Sharon who had got herself trapped in a bedroom with four men. Alone and half the height and weight of any of them, Malcolm boldy knocked on the door and demanded to see Sharon. Once the door opened Malcolm could see her sitting half naked and trembling on the edge of a bed. Four men stood between her and the door. 'Jesus loves Sharon and wants her to come home with me,' he said, staring the first youth in the eye. Seemingly without any fear, he walked across the room, instructing Sharon to get dressed quickly and walked out with her just seconds later.

A terrified young girl accompanied him home. It was only later that he himself went into shock, realising the potential danger that they had both been in. On another occasion, they received a young, severely abused Indian schoolgirl who had escaped home and family in fear of an arranged marriage. All of the men in her family descended upon Duke Street to take her home. Malcolm was left with the lonely task of defending her. Many of the girls had been abused physically, and nearly all were scarred emotionally. The majority had also become regular users of ouija boards or other forms of occult practice. Few had known stability or love in their young lives. Duke Street became a place of refuge for dozens and dozens of them in that first year. Some stayed a few nights, others weeks or months. Wherever possible Malcolm and Jennifer encouraged them to rebuild links with their families. Others just needed time and space to work out their problems. There was rarely a night when a bunk remained empty as the needs always outnumbered the beds. Malcolm and Jennifer knew that they were only scratching the surface and as time went on it wasn't only the plight of girls that became the focus of their concern.

The death of an ageing homeless man discovered lying in the back streets of Nuneaton in a cardboard box in the midst of newspapers and carrier bags shocked the whole town. His left hand had been eaten by rats. The front page headlines of the local paper described the circumstances graphically. Such details were no news to Malcolm, who regularly saw such sights and conditions. But the article had a drastic effect on him. He became desperate to provide some shelter for these men. Duke Street wasn't

the place, already too small for the work it had
to do, and they would never combine men and
girls in the same home. Malcolm began walking
the streets to find another place of refuge, this
time for men.

Ten

Midland and Oaston Roads

Like so many local authorities, Nuneaton Borough
Council struggled to provide support or make
adequate provision for homeless people in the
district. The temptation to pretend that there
wasn't a problem, was always there, until headlines in the local newspaper faced them with
something of the plight of these people. Part
of the problem lay in the fact that the people
with the power to influence change rarely saw
the conditions in which homeless people lived.
When such circumstances were brought to their
notice, as in the tragic case of the elderly man,
they were considered extreme, rare and blown
up by the press. But Malcolm knew differently.
There were more people living rough on the
streets than even he dared to think of, and the
most vulnerable were the elderly, mentally ill,
drug users and alcoholics. Any kind of shelter
found by these people would be extremely basic;
at best a derelict house and at worst a bus
shelter or porch entrance to a public building.
Newspapers, cardboard torn from supermarket
boxes or plastic carrier bags would become their

only protection from the cold night air. A few lucky ones might have acquired a blanket or two from a charity shop or refuse tip, but most were not so fortunate. Open fires, which frequently endangered not only their own lives but those of others living in nearby properties, were their only source of heat. Derelict buildings were especially dangerous places for the vulnerable homeless.

During the winter months and in severe weather conditions men would gather together, sleeping huddled in small groups, sheltering each other. Many suffered permanently with coughs, colds and other minor ailments but often some were more seriously ill. They would end up in the casualty department of the local hospital where they'd at least find warmth, comfort and appropriate treatment. Others would inevitably end up in cells at the local police station. Staff grew familiar with many of the characters and the sense of helplessness in their lives. Malcolm had no need to understand; he knew from first hand experience what it was like to feel rejected, desperate and alone in the world. Almost five years might have passed since he had walked the streets in search of accommodation and help, but the memory of those days remained crystal clear. He had been given a fresh chance, the opportunity to turn his back on the past and start again, and he longed to give these men the same. He knew that not one of them chose or wanted to live under these circumstances, and, given the opportunity, they could make something of their lives.

His task was somehow to provide that opportunity.

Number 3 Midland Road was owned by Nuneaton Borough Council. It was very run down and as far as Malcolm could see hadn't been occupied for some time. With improvements and redecoration he felt sure that it was the perfect place to accommodate homeless men. Before approaching the council, both he and Jennifer prayed. At first the council insisted that it couldn't release a property for this purpose, because the system prevented it. Despite having seen the value of the work at Duke Street and knowing the project at Midland Road was not likely to cost the council anything, councillors still couldn't see a way through the laws and regulations, though they did appear genuinely sorry. Malcolm had little patience with bureaucratic structures at the best of times, but on this occasion he was incensed by the red tape that was preventing them from occupying Midland Road. Then, rather quietly and off the record, somebody muttered something about how difficult and pointless it would be to remove anybody who might choose to occupy it. Malcolm took the hint, left quickly and started to make his plans.

At the St James Wednesday fellowship meeting that week he told them about Midland Road. A special time of praise and thanksgiving was offered to God for that wonderful provision, and together they committed the total needs of that project to God in prayer. Only a few months later Malcolm was informed that under a section of the Public Housing Act of 1936, number 3

Midland Road was now officially available as
a 'Common Lodging House'. Both the council
and the Worsleys were delighted. Prayer and
hard-working solicitors had won the day, moving
even borough councils.

With no time to waste Malcolm gathered around
him a group of Christian friends who both worked
and prayed about the house. It needed plumbing,
rewiring, redecorating and at a later date win-
dows were also replaced. Local churches donated
mattresses, furniture, pots and pans, clothing
and blankets, and within just a few weeks the
first six men came to live in Midland Road. The
conditions were deliberately basic but adequate.
Each came with his own tale, sad circumstances
and personal battles to face. Many were alcoholics, some drug users and others suffering from
some degree of mental illness. The majority had
at some stage been inside prison. The cards
were stacked against them, and life was pretty
bleak and dark wherever they looked. Midland
Road became a small but bright light in that
darkness strong enough for some to mark out
a new and positive future for themselves. Nothing delighted Malcolm more than to give them
that hope.

Midland Road operated an 'open door' policy
for twenty-four hours a day. Each man was
received and accepted for what he was, not
what he had been. Many were rejects from other
institutions, and nearly all came in straight
off the streets, where they might have been
'dossing' for some time. The rooms within the
house varied. Some were as basic as a mattress

on the floorboards, others had a bed, while one
was eventually carpeted and equipped with several items of furniture. Men were encouraged
to choose whatever degree of comfort they felt
happy with. Everyone was expected to pay a
minimum contribution to cover the cost of electricity, furniture, coal and crockery but they
were encouraged to organise the house themselves—even the rent collection. It would become
one man's responsibility to collect the money and
hand it over to Malcolm at the end of the week.
There was rarely an occasion on which a man
did not pay his way. The 'self-help' philosophy
was an important part of helping the men to
regain self-worth and discipline. Malcolm never
stayed on the premises for any length of time
and disliked the whole concept of staffed hostels.
Responsibility was placed upon them, and they
were left to work out the day-to-day running of
the house alone. As a result house rules emerged
from the men themselves and were enforced by
them! Inevitably newcomers were treated with
suspicion and indifference at first until they
showed some willingness to comply with the
rules, but in time they too grew to respect the
property, its contents and the trust placed upon
them. A local Christian even donated a colour
television, which in those days was considered
quite a luxury, and never once was it abused,
damaged or any attempt made to steal it.

Malcolm's role at Midland Road was critical, although he never appeared as a dominant
authoritive figure. Every day he walked to the
house ready to listen and help where he could.

The men were never quite sure what to make
of him, but as time went on it was his empathy,
not sympathy, that spoke the loudest. They
couldn't fail to recognise that he knew and
understood their suffering. His first-hand knowledge and experience of social services, probation
services and legal proceedings was invaluable.
He spent hours reading and interpreting complicated forms and leaflets. Many of them trusted
him with their sad life stories. He accompanied
those who were nervous and frightened of facing
'official' bodies or people and represented others
who were incapable of speaking for themselves.
Malcolm became their confidant and their 'arms',
'legs' and 'voice' when needed. By now his reputation with all of the official bodies in Nuneaton
was positive; they had grown to respect and
trust him. Earlier in the year, Geoff Ainsworth,
the director of Nuneaton Social Services, had
given him six months' casual work as a social
worker. Now, months later, he was still doing
much of the department's work although in an
unrecognised and unoffical capacity. Hours of his
time were spent in court, probation offices and
police stations. On a number of occasions he was
able to secure bail for some of the men, giving
them time and space to work through many of
their problems from Midland Road instead of a
police cell.

The ages and circumstances of each man varied considerably. Among the youngest came a
17-year-old who had already spent several years
in borstal. The authorities held out little hope for
his future with no family or friends to support or

encourage him each time he came out. Midland Road provided a base, people who understood, friends and space in which to stand back and reflect upon his circumstances. Nobody had ever offered him these things before. Over a period of months he regained some self-worth and confidence, started to apply for jobs and eventually rented a flat of his own. There was no greater satisfaction for Malcolm than to see the growth and development of this young man and others.

At the other end of the scale came a 67-year-old who, weary of life, simply wanted to die. With no living relatives or local authority help, he had ended up living on the streets. Malcolm found him, and Midland Road became his place of refuge. Months of negotiating and pushing finally secured him a place in a residential home for the elderly, where he ended his days with a degree of dignity and pride instead of becoming simply another statistic on the list of homeless deaths.

Caring for all of these men became a twenty-four hour job with very little time off for Malcolm or Jennifer. He promised them that whenever they needed him he would be there, whatever time of day or night it might be. Bob really tested his endurance. An alcoholic and depressive, as well as desperately insecure, he regularly rang Malcolm, threatening suicide. At varying times of the night and early hours of the morning Malcolm left his bed to sit with him, talking him through his trauma. The pattern repeated itself night after night until Malcolm became exhausted. 'Please, Bob, don't ring me tonight, You'll be all right, I know you will,' he pleaded. At

two'o'clock the following morning the telephone
rang. Malcolm groaned, and Jennifer begged him
not to go out again. The all-too-familiar voice
spoke on the other end, 'It's me Malcolm, Bob.
I'm just ringing to tell you you can stay in
bed. I'm all right. Don't worry about coming
out tonight as I'm not going to do anything
silly, I promise.' Fortunately God had given both
Malcolm and Jennifer a helpful sense of humour!

There were many stories of success and failure,
but the full impact of Midland Road upon men's
lives could never be calculated in quantitative
terms. It was impossible to measure the effects
of love, concern and compassion. Shelter, beds,
clothing and food were essential but temporary.
The Worsleys had something that would remain
long after the warm fire, hot meal and clean
clothes, but they knew it could never be forced
onto any one of them; each individual had to want
and choose it for himself. Their job was simply to
demonstrate it and, when invited, talk about the
hope and meaning to life that they had both found
through faith in God.

Some scoffed at the spiritual food available,
taking all the material and practical help they
could get, and then leaving. Others welcomed
talk about God and expressed a real interest for
a short time but were soon drawn back into the
false and temporary world of alcohol, drugs and
crime. But there were those who were genuinely
seeking for that which would change the direction of their lives, and many found it at Midland
Road. Keith was among the first and became a
source of real encouragement to Malcolm and

Jennifer as they saw this simple man change,
growing in love, faith and confidence.

Following the breakdown of his second marriage life seemed pretty meaningless for Keith.
With the help of a bottle of whisky and sleeping
tablets, he tried unsuccessfully to end it all.
It was soon after this that he was introduced
to Malcolm through a friend already living at
Midland Road. In the weeks and months that followed, Keith made three new friends; Malcolm,
Jennifer and God. Walking into their home,
playing with the children and being with them
as a family was like getting to know God. The
unseen person of Jesus was always present,
and Keith couldn't fail to notice. He was full
of faith and gratitude, doing everything he could
to improve conditions at Midland Road for all who
lived there. Shadowing Malcolm most of the time,
he became his right-hand man, learning all he
could from him in the process.

Within a year of their occupying number 3,
the borough council announced that the Worsleys
could also take over the house next door, provided
that it was improved to environmental health
standards. Keith carried out a lot of the work
on this property and started to take responsibility for the ever-increasing numbers of residents
within. He also found casual work as a gardener
and saved all but a few pounds of his wage,
determined one day to use it to make a new start
in life. That opportunity came, again through
Malcolm and Jennifer, sooner than he expected.

As well as numbers 3 and 5 Midland Road,
Duke Street continued to receive its endless

stream of teenage girls, many of whose problems
became far more difficult to handle than the
men's. Jennifer worked day and night to provide
a home for them, sharing not only the house,
food and possessions, but herself, her husband
and children. With both Paul and Helen growing
fast, they began to wonder how much longer
they could stay in the small terraced house.
Every week they were turning girls away because
of lack of space. Even though local Christian
groups were providing increased financial support, for Jennifer and Malcolm the possibility of
buying a larger property was out of the question. As always they took the problem to God
in prayer.

A couple of weeks later Malcolm received a
'phone call from the rural dean, the Reverend
David Jameson. An elderly lady from his congregation had recently died leaving a houseful of
furniture. The relatives wanted Malcolm to have
first refusal on the house contents for use at Duke
Street and Midland Road. It was a tremendous
offer, so he arranged to meet a relative of the
deceased woman at the house the following day.

The Oaston Road house was a dream. It had
five bedrooms, a large kitchen, two reception
rooms downstairs and two toilets! Malcolm's
mind was severely distracted from the furniture
he should have been looking at as he stood
trying to imagine what he and Jennifer could
do with a place like that. It would allow for a
little bit of family privacy, he thought. There
was even a self-contained unit within the house
where the girls could have a lot more space.

His imagination ran wild until in a typically forthright style Malcolm heard himself say to the relative, 'The house is nice. I don't suppose we could have that as well?' It was more a spoken dream than a serious question, for he knew full well they couldn't afford to rent or buy a house of this size. The response was not at all what he expected. He could hardly believe his ears as the reply came back very calmly, 'I don't see why not. We don't have any immediate plans for it.'

For once in their lives they were speechless. The second property at Midland Road had been an unexpected surprise, but this was more than they could ever ask or imagine. God had gone ahead, paving the way and supplying them with all that they needed to do his work. Malcolm and Jennifer were quick to share the good news with David Jameson, whose delight showed all over his smiling face. He was thrilled to have been able to play a small part in a big miracle. With thanks and praise in their heart, they made immediate plans to move.

Leaving Duke Street and all its memories was made easier by the delight of its new owner, Keith. For many months Jennifer had deposited his wage in a savings account for him, never imagining it would become the deposit for buying his own home. He loved every part of that building, having spent endless happy hours with the extended family there. Keith couldn't believe his ears when the Worsleys offered it to him, and in a short time he had obtained a mortgage. The grand move began; Keith from Midland Road to

Duke Street, the Worsleys from Duke Street to
Oaston Road.

The Worsleys were working flat out with hardly
any time to draw breath as the work both at
Oaston Road and Midland Road seemed to be
growing by the week. Malcolm was now responsible for three properties, with up to twenty
men and girls at any one time, as well as
continuing to carry out heavy preaching commit-
ments and work on the streets at night. Jennifer
was shattered and bore most of the weight of
the girls' problems. They existed from day to
day, never quite knowing where the next meal
would come from. The first winter it was the coal
that had run out, leaving the entire household
without any source of heat. Jennifer had reached
breaking point and demanded that Malcolm
do something about the problem immediately,
before the children died of the cold. Malcolm
prayed. As he prayed, the door bell rang, and
Jennifer went to answer it. David Carpenter, a
friend from St James, Weddington, stood on the
doorstep holding a gas fire and said, 'Is this any
good to you?' Within ten minutes Malcolm had
discovered a redundant gas pipe at the side of
the open fire and connected it up. The family said
their prayer of thanksgiving huddled around the
blissful heat.

In the last year Malcolm had been working
closely with a number of local Christians. They
supported the work prayerfully and financially,
but each of them knew that the time had come
for much greater structure and organisation if
it was all to be maintained. Malcolm needed

strong backing that would release him to continue the work at which he was gifted. He needed administrators, a secretary, a book keeper and accountant, legal advisors, a fund raiser, visitors and helpers for the hostels. The list seemed endless, and it all needed to come together as an official body that would give weight and recognition to the whole work.

As always it was important to Malcolm that these people should represent a wide range of denominations. He had no desire for any one church to adopt the project on its own; it had to be a corporate mission involving not only churches but local authorities and government bodies. Everyone has a responsibility towards homeless people, and he was determined to involve as many as he could in the task of bringing their needs before the whole community of Nuneaton. The Council of Churches became his first port of call in search of the backing he needed to continue this important work.

Eleven

Link Up

Guy Cornwall-Jones and David Jameson were both part of the small support group that had emerged over the previous two years. They shared with Malcolm the ecumenical vision for the project and were among the first to recognise the need for a more formal structure. Knowing Nuneaton Council of Churches, they felt it right to warn him that it was not the most exciting or visionary Christian body around. Its numbers and enthusiasm had dwindled over the years, and it had lost much of its sense of purpose and direction in that time. However, if anybody could inspire and motivate people, they were sure it was Malcolm, so they willingly accompanied him to the meeting.

Malcolm delivered his well-prepared speech describing graphically the conditions in which the homeless of Nuneaton lived, sparing few of the painful details. He told them the stories of Duke Street, Midland and Oaston Roads, the miracle of God's provision and the endless stream of men and girls who passed through their doors. He also told them of the ones they were forced to turn away through lack of funds, personnel and space. Finally, without reservation or apology, he asked the council to take the project under its wing, explaining the need for prayer, financial support and volunteers to assist the work. Malcolm made the commitment quite clear, stressing that it was a venture of faith, the future of which was totally in God's hands. If they agreed, he warned them, they'd be embarking on an unknown journey that would cost time, energy and money. He painted a full and realistic picture, hiding nothing.

A stunned silence followed Malcolm's delivery, each member of the council lost for words and hoping that another would be the first to respond. The ice was finally broken by a question; then others slowly started to express interest and concern, one or two even displaying a degree of enthusiasm. An hour or so of discussion followed about exactly what the council could do and how they might go about it. It was an enormous commitment, and while they could see the tremendous need and that God was clearly at the centre of it all, they were still daunted by the responsibility involved. Nobody found the courage to propose outright that they should agree to help; the best they could come up with was a conditional offer. They felt the need for a sign from God, some clear indication that it was right for them to take the project on, especially where the funding was concerned, as their financial resources were limited. Some members of the council left the meeting that night confident that the subject would not be

raised again. Others, including Malcolm, went
home to wait expecting God to work. Nor did
they have to wait long.

Unusually Jennifer was still up when Malcolm
got home to Oaston Road, and this time he could
see that she was awake with good reason. Far
from her usually sleepy state at that time of
night, she was pacing around the house smiling all over her face and clutching an envelope
in her right hand. He had barely got through
the door before she blurted out, 'Malcolm, it's
£1,000—more than we've ever received before.
Somebody just pushed it through the door tonight
with the message 'for your work with the homeless' written on the envelope.' Jennifer had no
idea of the details of that evening's meeting until
she watched Malcolm go straight to the 'phone
and ring the chairman of Nuneaton Council of
Churches. 'We've got our sign,' he said. 'Will
£1,000 do for starters?'

Motivation and enthusiasm among the Council
of Churches ran high following the 'sign' God had
given. They needed that encouragement, as much
of the work in the early stages proved boring
and tedious. The drawing up of a constitution,
appointment of trustees and officers and the
forming of a working committee took hours of
detailed planning. Registering the association
with the Charities Commission involved a solicitor and endless form filling. This lengthy process
taught Malcolm a great deal about administration and the need to do things right and in
order. Volunteers with a wide range of gifts and
abilities came forward at that time and, together

with Malcolm, successfully completed important
pioneering stages of the association.

'Link Up' was officially launched in March
1976, the name deliberately chosen to describe
the aim of the project—the linking together of
homeless men and girls with accommodation
and people who could care for them. It was
also a 'link up' of Christians from all the different denominations in the town. At the end of
the first year David Jameson, who had become
the first chairman, looked back on all that had
been achieved during this time. In his annual
report he wrote:

> This year we have necessarily been concerned
> a great deal with administration. But we must
> not forget that 'ministry' and 'administration'
> come from the same root word, which means
> 'serve'. The purpose of improving the admin-
> istration and putting it on a more permanent
> footing is that the personal ministering to
> people in need may be more effective. The work
> of Link Up is essentially a personal ministry. It
> is a matter of people meeting the urgent needs
> of other people. This is how it started, and this
> is how it must go on.

In one sense that first annual general meeting
was a dream come true for Malcolm. But in
another sense he was living every bit of the reality, working around the clock often seven days a
week in order to make the dream come true. In
less than a year Link Up had acquired offices

and appointed a part-time administrator and
secretary. For the first time since leaving Lindley
Lodge, Malcolm and Jennifer were receiving a
regular income paid by the Council of Churches.
A network of volunteer workers had been found
and trained to support both men and girls in
the various dwellings. A strong team of committed Christians made up the group of trustees
and working committee. Representatives came
from twelve different local churches spanning
eight denominations, all keen to pray, support
and keep their church members informed. An
advisory council made up of five professionals
from various supporting agencies was thrilled
and delighted to be included in this unusual
project. It seemed quite unbelievable, and it had
all happened alongside the day-to-day running of
Oaston and Midland Roads, which by then had
received 21 girls and 49 men respectively during
the first year.

The interest in Link Up spread far beyond
its workers and supporters as the local press
gave wide coverage, including photographs and
interviews with Malcolm, Jennifer and some of
the girls. Headlines such as 'Their Home for the
Homeless' and 'Church Project Means Another
Chance' captured the attention and imaginations
of local people and served to inform them about
the needs of the homeless living around them.
Professionally produced leaflets describing the
aims of Link Up were distributed throughout
the churches and placed in other strategic places
with a view to increasing support. All these and
other efforts were not in vain. Link Up emerged

as one of Nuneaton's most important charities,
whose work was being recognised both by ordinary people in the street and by the highest
officials in the local authority. Rotary clubs and
other fund-raising charitable organisations, local
industries and business people began to show
their support through gifts, donations, discounts
and sponsorship. Local authority grants were
made available for major building repairs, and
funding for workers through Manpower Services
schemes. Every stone was turned and avenue
explored for the sake of the homeless, and the
project went from strength to strength.

As the national problem of homeless people
grew during the 1970s, many local and central governments were spending huge sums of
money keeping the homeless in hotels or bed
and breakfast establishments. At the same time
there were thousands of empty houses, most
of them owned by local councils and awaiting
demolition. While shelter of some sort was being
provided, the real problems were being ignored.
Loneliness, isolation, breakdown in family relationships and the general despair among homeless people increased. Link Up emerged as a
small but unique organisation, succeeding where
other policies and ventures had failed. Some spe-
cialists were convinced that the total solution to
the problem of homelessness lay in such short-life
property schemes as Link Up's. 'Shelter' worker,
researcher and author Ron Bailey gave credit
to its success in his book *The Homeless and
the Empty Houses* (Penguin 1977), commending
its non-statutory approach and strong voluntary

basis. The strong Christian foundation on which
Link Up was built was also unique, but they were
only too pleased to share their experience and
ideas with any who wished to know. National
recognition by an expert in the field was something they had never sought or expected, but it
gave them increased courage and confidence to
continue the work they had begun.

As the workload increased, Malcolm and
Jennifer packed more and more into their days.
Being the only full-time employee meant that it
was important for Malcolm to attend as many
of the official meetings as he could, which often
broke into his evening work on the streets. But
they were never short of contacts and people
to fill the beds. Churches were taking their
own initiative, bringing men and girls to them
while the police, social workers and probation
officers were almost queueing up in the hope
that Malcolm could accommodate one of their
hopeless cases.

As well as the homes to oversee there was
the running of the offices at the George Eliot
Building in Nuneaton town centre. Pauline Gray
and Pat Kirkwood held the fort there as they
dealt with an endless stream of callers and
telephone enquiries, as well as providing the
secretarial back-up for the whole of Link Up.
But it didn't end there; what started out as
an enquiry and administration centre developed
into something much bigger than Malcolm had
ever envisaged.

In the first few months, 397 people had called
at the office with problems specifically relating

to homelessness. Some needed to be accommodated; some were in trouble with the police;
others sought advice on various benefits and
allowances for clothing, tools etc. In addition,
there had been a further 234 visitors, many of
whom were volunteering their practical help,
prayers and encouragement. A few looked for
guidance and counselling on other matters not
related to homelessness. It was just the tip of
the iceberg, and it became obvious to Malcolm
that the workload had to be shared even more
widely. One of the most important tasks for him
now was the training and equipping of others to
work with him.

In an attempt to do this he wrote and produced a manual called 'Link Up Procedure, Law
and Policy'. It contained every possible piece of
information necessary for helping the homeless,
from current law and criminal legal procedures,
to where to find second-hand clothing and fill out
forms for Link Up residents. All telephone numbers of supportive doctors, hospital staff, probation
and social workers and volunteers were listed.
This manual thus served as an important training and information document for the volunteer
workers. From time to time they would all come
together to discuss their various experiences and
learn from each other. Malcolm encouraged and
assisted wherever he could.

An increasing amount of time was being taken
up with various kinds of small group work at
the George Eliot Building. Malcolm was already
running small groups for alcoholics, drug users
and those seeking rehabilitation. It made sense

to bring together several people struggling with
the same problems rather than spending hours
and hours talking with individuals. While he had
a fair amount of personal experience to share, he
knew that the greatest impact would come from
the men themselves. And it was men like Keith
Doughty who had that impact.

Meanwhile Jennifer carried the burden of the
day-to-day running of Oaston Road. Getting the
girls to accept responsibility for their own lives
was hard work. Few looked for jobs, and those
who had them struggled to get themselves there
every day. When they did, it was rarely on time.
The many pregnant girls needed basic education
on health and diet as well as preparation for
the birth of their babies. They were often reluctant to attend ante-natal classes, so the bulk of
their help came from Jennifer. With no support
from friends or family, two of the younger girls
pleaded with her to be with them throughout the
birth. She was. Jennifer became the mother that
so many of them had lacked. She was always
there when they needed her, listening, caring,
encouraging and supporting. Above all she gave
them love.

Under the new Link Up structures Jennifer
had also been officially appointed as assistant
treasurer, which involved her in hours of book-
keeping late into the night after Helen and Paul
had gone to bed. Life was full, too full, and the
strain began to show on the Worsley household.
Jennifer had already sought help from a local
Anglo-Catholic priest a year earlier. In desperation she begged him to talk Malcolm into slowing

down and spending a little more time with her and the children. She was beginning to feel like the last person on his list of needy people—as if she were a single parent herself.

Malcolm had been surprised to see Father David waiting for him one night when he eventually arrived home. They had not always seen eye to eye on their understanding of gospel presentation, and Malcolm felt sure that this priest must have called to get 'converted'. God couldn't have chosen a more appropriate man to humble him as he began to see that this godly man was practising exactly what Malcolm was only pretending to do—love his neighbour *and* his wife! For a while Malcolm had made a concerted effort to take time off, but the demands a year later were almost doubled. It finally took a bout of illness and a near fatal accident to make both of them stop and rethink their priorities of work and home, for these had become unhealthily blurred in the last year or so. Fortunately Malcolm was at home when the accident occurred.

Helen was a healthy, active two-year-old who had been walking steadily for some time and, like most small children, loved the adventure of stairs. Oaston Road was a child's paradise with its many doors, rooms and steps, and interior alterations had created a few more than would normally be found in the average family home. On this occasion she escaped from the room where she had been playing happily under the watchful eye of mother and brother. Only seconds later there came a noise rather like cannons firing several shots in close succession. It was

the sound of Helen's small body somersaulting
downwards, hitting every single step on the tall,
narrow staircase as she fell. Jennifer reached the
bottom first and screamed for Malcolm, who was
somewhere outside in the garden. The two bent
over the motionless body. Helen was limp and
colourless. Her lips turned purple, and she had
stopped breathing. Malcolm instructed Jennifer
to send for an ambulance but then stopped her
saying, 'No, let's pray.' With eyes closed and
hearts beating fast, they laid their hands on
Helen's head and body. Unable to find the words
he needed, Malcolm cried and groaned to God in
anguish and desperation for his daughter's life.
Minutes passed, and neither of them dared to
look, in case what they saw confirmed their
worst fears. As he knelt in the silence Malcolm
sensed an unusual warmth come into his hands,
as if he was immersing them in warm water.
It felt hotter and hotter, travelling up his arms
and into Helen's body. Still with eyes closed he
continued to speak to God in his own personal
prayer language for several more minutes. It was
only the movement in Helen's body that caused
him to stop and open his eyes. It was the most
beautiful and precious sight he had ever seen
before or since. Her eyes were open, little face
smiling and cheeks glowing. She sat up and then
jumped to her feet, looking at her parents rather
blankly and wondering why they were kneeling
on the hallway floor. Within seconds Helen ran
off to find her toys.

Malcolm and Jennifer were convinced that
Helen was a walking miracle and could barely

believe what they had just witnessed. But being
so close to tragedy made them stop and think
about their lifestyle and the pressures upon
them as a family. The children were growing
up fast. Paul would soon be going to school and
Helen to nursery, and their needs and stages in
life demanded more structure and routine. Since
receiving a regular income and having sold the
house on Duke Street they had managed to get a
mortgage on a small property in Blackpool, which
became their bolthole on days and occasional
weekends off. But this was clearly not enough.
Members of the council were also expressing
concern for their health and well-being. It was
obvious that both were in danger of burning
themselves out. On an infrequent visit to the
doctor at this time, Malcolm was asked if he had
any money. Somewhat confused by the question,
he said that they had a little. His GP said, 'Fine!
Book yourselves a holiday today, and if you are
not out of the country by the end of the week I
am putting you into hospital!' Four days later the
four of them were in Majorca.

The break gave them time to reflect and pray
about their commitment to Link Up. Perhaps
their dream had been fulfilled? They had been
God's instruments in setting up an interdenominational organisation that was meeting the needs
of homeless people in Nuneaton. Had their part
in it all come to an end. Was their job complete?
Maybe it was time to hand over the work to those
with different gifts who could take the project a
stage further along the road in God's plan? The
questions went round and round in their heads

for some time before they reached a decision. But when it was finally made, they had a peace and assurance that it was the right one.

As was the case when they left Lindley Lodge, they felt God calling them out again. Where exactly they would go, what they would do and how they would tell the people of Link Up, they didn't know. But it was definitely time to move on.

Twelve

Moving On

It wasn't easy telling the trustees of their decision to leave Link Up. Their time together had been hard work, and they had grown very close as a team. Malcolm and Jennifer felt partly that by leaving they would be breaking up a family. Undoubtedly all would feel a tremendous sense of bereavement. In a way, the situation was eased slightly because David Jameson had announced his intention to finish as chairman only a few weeks earlier, so the wind of change had already begun to blow. But the news still came as a terrible shock to some members of the committee, who had never imagined Link Up without the Worsleys. In their minds the two were inseparable.

Jennifer and Malcolm allowed a suitable lapse of time between the announcement and their departure to enable the committee to fill the gap. They knew the job would need to be advertised and interviews arranged, all of which was new territory for the trustees and would take time. They continued to encourage and support wherever they could, but their tiredness was

quite obvious to people now. There had been
moments in the last few months when their
faith had felt as weak as their bodies, and it
was sheer discipline that kept them going. They
prayed earnestly that God would provide Link
Up with their successors and show them the
direction they should take. It was at times like
these that Malcolm was grateful for the new
structures that had enabled the burden of Link
Up to be shared, and he knew that he could
now depend on the faith and prayers of a whole
group of people.

One area of work he had especially enjoyed
pioneering was the support groups for alcoholics. Classified as an alcoholic himself, he felt
confident and able to empathise with the suf-
ferers' condition. Withdrawal and rehabilitation
had been hard enough for him, even with the
restraint of Haverigg and support of his friends
at Lindley Lodge, and he still lived with the
scars. Malcolm knew the uphill struggle in front
of those men and did everything that he could
to help them fight their illness. The results from
his group work were encouraging. Several had
succeeded in giving up their drinking and were
in turn supporting others. It was an exciting
and challenging venture for Malcolm, one he
knew he would be sorry to leave behind. Wherever God guided him, he hoped and prayed to
be able to use the lessons and experiences of
his past to the full. He waited patiently and
was not disappointed.

Langley House Trust is a Christian charitable organisation concerned for the aftercare

of ex-prisoners. The trust has many hostels
scattered around the country which serve as
halfway houses for men coming out of prison.
The Lancaster-based hostel was especially concerned for elderly men who remained homeless
after their sentences. Many had severe drinking
problems, and the trust was looking for someone
to pioneer a specialist unit within the hostel for
alcoholics. The job came with a reasonable salary
and a house. It held the title of warden and was
brought to Malcolm's attention by a social worker
friend. Following a visit and interview, the trust
was delighted to offer him the position. With their
house not too far away in Blackpool and easily
accessible for weekends off, they felt confident
that the move was right. Meanwhile the Link Up
trustees had interviewed and appointed Dick and
Muriel Bates to take over Malcolm and Jennifer's
job. Things seemed to be coming together well,
and God was surely answering their prayers.

   There were many arrangements to be made
for the children, who were now at school and
nursery, as well as furniture and belongings to
pack. Jennifer was weary and wondered how
she was going to cope with the next few weeks'
emotional trauma of saying goodbye and moving
to Lancaster. Fortunately there were fewer girls
at Oaston Road to worry about as two were about
to go to Spain on holiday—a gift given them
by one of the Link Up prayer partners as a
reward for their effort and hard work during the
year. But right at the last minute there was a
problem. With only a few hours to go before their
departure, one of the girls could not be found.

Passports, tickets and luggage were waiting, but
Sharon was nowhere in sight.

The problem was easily resolved in Malcolm's
eyes—Jennifer could go in her place. He would
have the children and make all the necessary
arrangements for moving if she would take the
break she so obviously needed. She laughed at
the suggestion, knowing full well that she had
already packed her summer clothes and passport
and taken them to the house in Blackpool. That
didn't change Malcolm's mind. Within minutes
he was in the car making the two-hour journey
to Blackpool with the intention of bringing back
all that Jennifer needed for a holiday. Less than
six hours later she was on board a bus to Spain,
completely disorientated but too exhausted to
object. During the journey she spilt a flask of
boiling coffee all over her thigh, leaving her with
a serious burn. The entire holiday was spent
resting in the shade. It was a God-enforced rest
that proved vital in preparation for what became
a very difficult six months in Lancaster.

The first disappointment came when the house
that they had been promised by Langley House
Trust turned out to be a small two-bedroomed
flat on the top floor of the hostel. Cramped living
conditions and the residential work pressures
were equal to Oaston Road and to everything
they had sought to leave behind. Still feeling
a little fragile from the last few years and not
wanting to create a fuss at the start of their new
job, Malcolm and Jennifer moved in and tried
to make the best of a difficult situation. But
further blows followed when residents burgled

them, stealing some of Jennifer's jewellery and her bike. Other items of enormous sentimental value were also taken. Then they discovered that they were not covered by the trust's insurance. All this didn't help them to settle.

Sadly the work with the alcoholics also had its frustrations. Because the vision for a unit had come from the central committee and not from the local working body, Malcolm felt the conflicts between colleagues who had very different ideas about working with the men. Pressures came to bear upon them to pursue an alternative line of work than that they had both felt Malcolm had been employed to do, and so rather than compromise their convictions, they made the very difficult decision to resign. While serving their notice they made arrangements to move to their house in Blackpool and face the future there. How they would pay the mortgage they were not sure.

Frank Rice was the local liaison probation officer for the Langley Trust Hostel. Based in Lancaster, he visited clients there regularly and got to know Malcolm and Jennifer well in that time. He liked Malcolm's ideas and recognised the unique experience and abilities of this man. Hearing of his resignation, Frank arranged for Malcolm to see a colleague who was responsible for setting up a new probation hostel near Blackpool.

Hoole House in Elswick used to be an old isolation hospital surrounded by sixteen acres of beautiful grounds, and Duncan Brown was the senior probation officer responsible for its

opening as a probation hostel. Malcolm knew
nothing about the man or his ideas for working
with men and after the Lancaster experience
was naturally cautious about accepting any job
lightly. But on this occasion his respect for Frank
was sufficient for him to want to pursue it as
a possibility. They arranged to meet at Hoole
House. Only minutes into their conversation,
Duncan looked up at Malcolm and said, 'I'm
a committed Christian and I'm looking for a
team who will work with me upholding Christian
principles. How do you feel about that?' For a
few seconds Malcolm was lost for words; not a
common problem for him. He quickly recovered,
and the two men spent the next few hours
exchanging ideas, experiences and exploring the
realistic possibility of Malcolm becoming assistant warden for the hostel.

The disappointment of the last six months
drifted into the background as the Worsleys
made plans to live permanently, for the first
time since they had bought it, in their Blackpool
house. Jennifer dared not get too excited about
the prospect of having a normal family home
for the first time in their married life and a
husband who went to work like other men, just
in case something should go wrong. But this
time it didn't, and Malcolm thrived on the challenge and stimulation of working alongside probation officers at Hoole House. They in turn
grew to value and appreciate the unique experience and understanding that he had of the men
who lived there. In fact the deputy chief of the
Lancashire Probation Service was so impressed

with Malcolm's work that he invited him to
discuss the possibility of full-time training within
the probation service.

Harry Rooney was convinced that the Probation Service needed men like Malcolm Worsley
and was quite prepared to use his weight and sen-
iority to pave the way for him to be accepted for
training. Both men knew that Malcolm's prison
record was the only, but enormous, obstacle in
the way and a little bit of research revealed that
every application from an ex-convict in the past
had failed miserably. Malcolm was quite sure
that there was no hope; why should his case
be considered any different from the others,
and there was every chance that his record was
much longer than most. But Harry persisted,
and, promising his full support and backing,
persuaded Malcolm to submit an application for
a two-year CQSW course with view to training
as a probation officer. He waited for the rejection
slip to arrive.

London-franked letters were rare in the Worsley
household, least of all those with the Home Office
printed on the envelope. The very official-looking
document invited him to attend a special interview with the Chief Inspector of Probation in
connection with a recent application for training
within the probation service. Harry Rooney was
the only one not surprised by the news.

Malcolm felt rather numb and, having never
expected to get beyond a rejection slip, slightly
nervous and daunted at the prospect of an interview at the Home Office. It was with mixed
emotions that he travelled down to London, not

wanting to build up his hopes, but also fearing
what he knew would be a feeling of rejection
should he fail to be accepted. God had promised
him a future of hope and purpose, but he knew
that the promise didn't spare him from these
difficult moments when he had to learn to trust.

It was a highly skilled interview, thorough, and
with its tense moments. Malcolm had decided
to take it slowly and honestly. Even if he had
wanted to, there was no way he could outwit
these chaps. They'd been interviewing people
all their lives. So he sat back and gave the most
honest account of his life that he could, which of
course included his Christian testimony. But by
the time he got on the train home later that day
he could recall nothing; his mind had gone blank
with sheer exhaustion.

At the end of the longest two weeks of their
lives, the second letter from the Home Office
eventually arrived. Jennifer and Malcolm both
stood staring at it with disbelief. History was in
the making: in spite of his criminal record, he had
been accepted for social work training with a view
to becoming a probation officer. Not only that, but
they were prepared to give him a full grant and
generous book allowance, plus full expenses for
the course. There was also the prospect of a job
waiting for him at the end. Malcolm spent the
next few weeks thanking God, Harry Rooney,
Duncan Brown and Hoole House for making an
impossible dream come true.

Studying was no problem to Malcolm. Since
prison days he had continued to work at one or
another correspondence course and had found

great satisfaction in using the brain that had
lain dormant for so long. The chance to read and
study a subject of which he had so much practical
first-hand experience excited him intellectually.
But the course was also stimulating practically,
calling for several weeks' placement when stu-
dents were expected to fulfil a wide range of social
and probation work practices. A few weeks before
they were to go out, the college principal asked to
see Malcolm in his office.

'I've been taking a great interest in your work,
Malcolm, and I've decided that you are living
with a ghost in your life and I want to help you
get rid of it.' Malcolm didn't need the statement
explained; he was all too aware that he was living
with his prison record on his shoulder. It was a
psychological battle that had resurfaced when he
started college, and he was struggling to get rid
of it. He welcomed his tutor's invitation of help
but wasn't quite prepared for the suggestion
that followed.

'I've arranged for you to do your first-year
residential placement at Lancaster Prison, working alongside the probation officer there. It's all
cleared with the governor. You've got to go into
prison next year as part of your probation office
placement, so I suggest you face it now before
that time arrives.'

Nervous, but confident that he was going with
the backing of the college and the prayers of
many people, Malcolm stood outside the forbidding doors of the Lancaster jail. The all-too-
familiar bell rang, and a prison officer opened
the door. He delivered his well-rehearsed speech:

'I'm Malcolm Worsley, student in training for probation work, and am reporting for placement duty within the prison.' He handed the officer the official college letter verifying his position. It was only when the letter wasn't automatically taken that he looked more closely at the man and read the expression of disbelief and horror in his eyes.

'Why do you say you are here?' the prison officer asked him for the second time, only now with a harsh note in his voice.

'I'm a probation student and have come to work here for the next six weeks,' Malcolm mumbled.

'Not in this bloody prison, you're not,' the man said and slammed the door in his face. It was his landing officer from Walton Prison.

The devastation was indescribable. How he made the journey home to Jennifer and faced the college he didn't know. There were moments in the next few days when he wondered if he would ever recover.

God had used many different people to support Malcolm through the years, but there was no doubt that the members of his college tutor group became his mainstay at this time, both individually and corporately. They sensitively and perceptively led him through the trauma, restoring pride and dignity to his crushed spirit. The prison governor was informed about the incident and later invited him into the prison to receive an apology. Alternative arrangements were made for him to work in a nearby rehabilitation centre for physically handicapped men and women.

Two years came quickly to an end, and the delight of being a fully qualified social worker helped the negative memories of the prison incident to fade into the background. Lancashire Probation Service offered Malcolm a job in its Fleetwood office, just a few miles from their new home in Carleton. With Paul and Helen enjoying their new school and Jennifer finding a part-time teaching job, everything was coming together well for the Worsley household. Malcolm was really beginning to believe that he was 'normal' and could lead a normal life like any other family man. They spent the next ten years doing just that.

Thirteen

The In-between Years

The Old Testament character Joseph had more than a fair share of high drama in life, so much so that he became a good subject for the popular musical *Joseph and his Technicolor Dreamcoat*. Most people are able to recall his colourful coat, dreams, attempted murder, prison sentences and later his rise to power and fame, as well as the dramatic way in which he was restored to his alienated family. But few will remember the details of the years between these two worlds, when he was slowly and steadily growing as a person, rebuilding a shattered life and restoring piece by piece the self-worth and confidence that had been squashed out of him by his jealous and cruel brothers. These were the silent years of growth that made him the man who was able to lead a nation through trauma and crisis and receive lovingly without bitterness or resentment the family who had earlier rejected him. Thousands of years may separate the lives of Joseph and Malcolm, but God's handling of them both in the middle phases of their lives is similar. Neither knew what the future would hold, but both had turned their backs on the past and were determined to move on.

Malcolm had already made enormous strides, far beyond all he could ever have hoped or imagined. But deep inside there were things that he had to prove to himself. Failure still haunted him, and even though he was assured of God's forgiveness, somehow Malcolm couldn't forget. He longed to reconcile parts of his past with the present, bringing healing and wholeness into many relationships and circumstances. Despite the training, qualifications, and the job he now held, nothing would convince him that he was 'normal'. Only time would tell whether he was capable of maintaining a stable, secure lifestyle that fulfilled responsibilities to his wife, children, employers and society. For his own peace of mind he had to succeed where in the past he had failed so miserably.

At work in the Fleetwood office only Malcolm's boss officially knew the details of his past. It was considered unnecessary for everyone on the staff to know, something Malcolm appreciated enormously. It was so important for him to be able to build up good, strong, healthy and 'normal' working relationships without feeling people were either hiding prejudice, making exceptions for him or taking pity on him. He wanted to be accepted and appreciated in his own right, on the basis of his personality now, not in relation to what he had been in the past. Maintaining those relationships over an extended period was critical for him to believe in himself and in his abilities and skills as a probation officer. Working

as part of a team, recognising and releasing
each other's gifts, was also an important part
of this growth process. But he need not have
been anxious, for what God had begun he was
very definitely going to bring to completion.

Within a short space of time Malcolm had
gained the respect and recognition of his colleagues. Not only did he fulfil the work require-
ments, but he pioneered new ground in his
work with young offenders, setting patterns
which others would follow. In an attempt to
keep these boys and youths out of borstals
and detention centres Malcolm developed and
led outdoor activity weeks that would challenge
them physically, mentally and emotionally. Many
discovered depths of character they didn't know
they had and which in time gave them the
determination and strength needed to keep out
of trouble, especially out of prison. Often Malcolm
went beyond the bounds of duty, spending additional weekends taking youngsters away on hostel and camping trips up into the Lake District.
It became a family activity involving Jennifer
and the children, their corporate lives once more
influencing those who had little or no experience
of family love and security.

In time their joint, relatively high and stable
income enabled them to buy a rather small,
dilapidated terraced cottage in the Lake District.
It needed vast amounts of work before it could be
enjoyed to the full, so many weekends were spent
knocking parts down and rebuilding. Once more
Malcolm's building skills were put to full use. The
Waingate cottage became their place of refuge, a

holiday home for friends, family and colleagues.
It was no surprise to those who knew them to
discover that the cottage was in Haverigg, just
a few hundred yards from the entrance to the
prison drive. Each time they went there, Malcolm
pinched himself just to make sure that he wasn't
dreaming and that he really was the owner of
two properties. God was teaching him how to
be that good steward—for which Shirley Marsh
had set the example so many years before at
Lindley Lodge. Their simple lifestyles had barely
changed, but God was teaching them to put their
extra earnings to wise use. Their homes were
their places of ministry, and many were sent
into their lives in this way.

The vicar of the local church where they worshipped in Carleton was one of the few who knew
of Malcolm's chequered history. To the average onlooker, especially neighbours, they were
simply a lovely friendly young family who worked
hard in their professions and homes. Helen and
Paul attended the local primary school, and
together they worshipped at the village church.
Once settled in his new job, Malcolm took up
his lay readership, assisting in the leading of
worship and occasionally preaching.

Carleton Church was quite different from where
he had worshipped previously. The churchman-
ship was Anglo-Catholic and the style of worship
new to him, but he didn't allow that to stop
him from becoming a much loved and valued
member of the fellowship. Unity between and
within the denominations was always one of
Malcolm's priorities, and here was a further

opportunity for him to display his yearning for
oneness in the faith. In an attempt to draw people
together, he embraced different spiritual traditions and accommodated varying styles of worship but never moved from his strong stand on
personal salvation and new life in Christ. God
used him to encourage many in that faith, not
least through their fortnightly Bible studies at
home and the young people's group. But at no
point did he feel free or led by God to give
his own powerful testimony and, in contrast
to his time in Nuneaton, there were no invitations to go out speaking at other evangelistic
rallies and events. Life took on a very different
routine and perspective. Normal working hours
released time and space for Malcolm to discover
delights he had missed completely in earlier
life. Jennifer thrived on their stable family life,
enjoying the security of routine, and pursuing her
own career as a full-time teacher. She continued
to encourage and support Malcolm in his pursuit
of 'normality'. From time to time their bungalow
would be littered with the evidence of his latest
hobby, the phase which most people go through
in adolescence but which Malcolm had never
entered. One week it would be stamp collecting;
the next, playing golf or painting; then photography; and after that bird watching. Each interest
would totally absorb his surplus energy as he
endeavoured to cram into a few weeks the many
years he had lost as an alcoholic and criminal.
He followed many of the children's interests with
them, strengthening the bonds he had barely
felt with his first two sons, Stephen and Alan.

Attending school assemblies, open days, parents'
evenings, concerts and standing on the touch
line of the local football pitch watching young
Paul earn his place in the school team were
important events in the process of restoration.
God had given him another chance, and Malcolm
was a father in the making, learning daily how
to love, support and encourage his children. It
was so important to him that he gave them his
best, all he had and more. His failure with Alan
and Stephen still hurt and, ironically, the more
he proved to himself that he could now be a
responsible parent, the more it pained him that
he had let his first two sons down.

There were painful moments when his mind
would turn back nearly ten years to a particular
day inside Haverigg Prison. A prison officer had
ushered him into the interview room informing
him that he had a visitor. The social worker
sitting at the desk was unknown to him and
quite unexpected. And the news that he gave
was an even greater shock: Josephine, Malcolm's
first wife, had met another man. They intended
to marry, and she wanted Malcolm to sign the
adoption forms allowing her new husband to
become legal guardian of Alan and Stephen. He
had less than half an hour in which to decide.
Their divorce had somehow been relatively pain-
less, as Malcolm realised only too well that he
couldn't expect Josephine to forgive him for the
dreadful things he had done. He knew he had
to release her to a new life. But even though he
had not seen the two boys for some time, actually
sitting there trying to decide whether he should

sign them away to another man was already a
nightmare. He was their father and always would
be; no one could ever alter that fact, but having
become a Christian he was also very conscious of
his failure as a father.

He wrestled within himself, staring blankly at
the social worker whose job it was to get the forms
signed. He knew that by not signing he was being
selfish. At that time he thought it unlikely that
he would ever be in a position to offer them a
stable home in which to grow up, but here was
a man who could. Bert had been part of Alan and
Stephen's lives since they were three and one
year old respectively. For their sakes Malcolm
began to see the sense in it all, however painful
it might be for him.

An added complication was that Bert planned
to take them all to South Africa to live, where
they would have the chance to get away from the
pain of the past and start again. It was unlikely
he would ever see them again. He had no way
of telling them he loved them, and no way of
guaranteeing that his signature on those forms
wouldn't be interpreted as 'I don't want you'. Yet
nothing could be further from the truth. It was
the love of a father that released them to a far
better way of life than he could offer at that time.
It was love which let them go. It had been one of
the hardest things he had ever had to do and was
still surfacing painfully ten years later.

Alan and Stephen were never far from Malcolm's
thoughts and prayers during these years, but
his sense of failure always prevented him from
trying to establish contact with them. Even if

he had found the courage, he wouldn't have
known where to begin finding them. It was
therefore quite a shock to discover 'coincident-
ally' while in casual conversation with friends
one day that someone bearing the name of his
ex mother-in-law lived very close by in Preston.
A nervous 'butterfly' feeling inside him somehow
told him that it was undoubtedly Betty. After
much thought, prayer and deliberation, he made
the decision to ask a good friend to visit Betty and
tell her something of Malcolm's life since leaving
Haverigg and to ask if he might call to see her.
It was more from a state of disbelief, shock and
curiosity that she agreed to a meeting than from
a genuine desire to see Malcolm, but a time and
date was agreed.

The first half hour was awkward and difficult
as Betty and Malcolm sat staring at each other
in a state of disbelief. He said very little, waiting
for her to speak. Gradually she began to bring to
the surface the horrific memories of the earlier
years of his life. It was a painful period of time,
but he knew he had to sit and listen. There were
things he himself couldn't remember or perhaps
had chosen to forget, but at no point did he try to
defend or justify himself. The look on his face and
the way in which he sat said it all—'I'm guilty
and deserve nothing.' The visit was the first
of several carefully arranged meetings where
together they worked through some of the painful
times of the past and built a relationship on
new ground. It took some time for Betty to
adjust to the new Malcolm. She didn't believe
in miracles, yet she knew she was looking at one.

As time went on she melted under the warmth
and love she was now experiencing in place of
the selfishness she had once known in him. They
were destined to meet far more frequently than
either of them ever expected, as each discovered
the other owned a holiday cottage in Haverigg.
How—other than God's divine planning—they
had never bumped into each other in the tiny
two-shop village they did not know! A piece of
the jigsaw in Malcolm's past had been delicately
replaced by his Master Builder, and he walked
one more step along the path of wholeness.

It was Betty who restored the link between
Malcolm and his sons, her grandsons. Much
prayer and thought went into the letters he
wrote them in South Africa. He asked for nothing
other than an opportunity to explain why he felt
he had to sign their adoption papers. Their
replies were more than he could have hoped for,
especially from Alan, the eldest, who had some
very real memories of his father. It was the start
of a long process of catching up between father
and sons that continues to this day. As married
men with families of their own, they were able
to understand something of the bonds between
parents and children, however far apart they
might have been. Those bonds were emotionally
renewed just a few years later when Stephen
came home to visit his father, Jennifer, Paul
and Helen in Carleton. Father and son spent a
wonderful few days together walking in the Lake
District, getting to know each other and building
the foundations for their future relationship.

Malcolm knew that he couldn't undo the past

or try to compensate for it but should, as he
had done with Betty, work through as much of
the past as he could and build on new ground.
It was important for his new family that he
didn't dwell on the negative details of bygone
years but that Alan and Stephen saw him as
the man he now was and were able to receive
Jennifer and the children as part and parcel of
their father's life. Jennifer had been scared of
meeting Malcolm's first two children, not only
for herself but for Helen and Paul also. They had
some knowledge of their father's past, but not in
great detail. In the end she need not have feared.
Stephen's departure at the end of his visit was
surrounded with tears from everybody, and firm
promises were made for both Helen and Paul to
visit them in South Africa as soon as the funds
could be found. Two years later they spent three
wonderful weeks with their half brothers, their
wives and families.

Meeting Josephine when she was on holiday
with her mother in Preston was not quite such
a smooth experience. The hurt inside her went
understandably deep and was compounded by
the recent breakdown of her second marriage.
She had heard about Malcolm's new life, new
wife and children from her mother, Betty; but
in many ways this news had intensified her
pain and anguish, and their meeting provided
her with an opportunity to give vent to many of
those feelings. Malcolm stood and took as much
as he was able to take, knowing full well that
he had no defence. Eventually he walked away,
paralysed by the painful knowledge of the deep

hurt and pain that he alone had inflicted on one
woman. It was some time before he could even
pray about that meeting, and he secretly hoped
there would not be another.

Josephine's third son, born to her second husband, was called Peter. Following the breakdown
of his parents' marriage he had come to live
with his grandmother in Preston, spending much
of his spare time in Haverigg at one of the
other cottages on Waingate. Nobody was more
surprised than Malcolm to see him standing at
the cottage door one day asking if he might
come in and talk. It was the first of many
hours spent with Peter in Haverigg as they
forged a strong friendship together. Malcolm
became the father figure Peter had missed so
desperately in the later stages of his growing
years. The family circle was widening, and its
base was increasingly in Haverigg.

With Peter now living in England permanently,
Josephine made regular trips to visit both her son
and mother. She had heard about Malcolm's links
with Peter, although her next encounter with him
had not been planned. Haverigg's main street
was not large and without appearing extremely
rude one couldn't avoid another person walking
by. Malcolm and Josephine met head on. He froze
on the spot, hardly daring to breathe for fear of
the pain he felt sure he was about to experience.
Josephine's eyes were softer and her voice calm
as she spoke. 'Thank you for helping my mother,
Malcolm, and for spending time with Peter. It's
appreciated very much, especially with me being
so far away.' To Malcolm they were words of

healing and perhaps in God's time and by his
grace he might be forgiven by Josephine. He
felt he had no right to ask but silently hoped
and prayed.

Healing and wholeness in Haverigg was becoming quite a regular feature of the Worsleys' lives
during this time. Their cottage was now in full
use, and much of their holiday time and weekends
were spent there growing together as a family.
The probation work in Fleetwood continued to be
a challenge and real encouragement to Malcolm.
Life was good, fulfilling and very happy. The
Worsleys could see no reason why it shouldn't
continue that way for the rest of their lives . . .
until a passing comment in the staff room during
a coffee break stirred up in Malcolm that strange
feeling that he had experienced so many times in
the past when he was being moved on. But on this
occasion it was more like being moved home.

Fourteen

Back to Haverigg

'Hey, Malcolm, there's a job going at Haverigg Prison. Why don't you apply for it? It's just what you need, and you could go and live in your cottage.'

The speaker was one of Malcolm's colleagues, who was sitting on a desk browsing over the job advertisements while drinking coffee. There was no great flash of lightning or clap of thunder with a voice from heaven saying, 'Malcolm Worsley, I call you from Fleetwood to the probation department of Haverigg Prison.' Far from it. In fact he can't remember giving his colleague any kind of meaningful reply. He simply grunted something like, 'Oh, really?' But inside a disturbing feeling welled up. For some years he hadn't experienced it, but now it had surfaced again, and he recognised it immediately.

At home later that night he told Jennifer about the job and tested her with the possible thought of applying. 'Do you think Haverigg would have me back as a probation officer?' he asked. Jennifer knew better than to dismiss the impossible where Malcolm was concerned

and simply said, 'Well, you could always try.
What have you got to lose?' On the surface
Malcolm had nothing to lose. He'd got a good
job, salary and a healthy family life. Failing to
get the Haverigg position wouldn't change any
of that. And yet something bothered him deeply.
In the likely event of failure, could he take what
would undoubtedly be a knock to his pride? And
dare he risk bringing to the surface further hurt
and pain stemming from his time in Haverigg?
These were big questions to be faced before he
could even send off for an application form.

Malcolm decided to seek advice, especially from
his colleagues, whose opinions he valued greatly.
He talked through the realistic possibility of applying for the job with the senior probation officer
at Fleetwood, fully expecting her to laugh at the
idea. On the contrary, she both encouraged him
and promised a good reference. That, together with
the wisdom and prayers of Christian friends, gave
him the confidence he needed to complete the form.
Within a few weeks his references had been taken
up, and he was offered an interview.

Ian Lockwood, Haverigg's governor, made no
attempt to hide his astonishment on hearing of
Malcolm's record. 'I'm sorry, Mr Worsley. If I
had known you had a criminal record, you would
never have been short-listed, never mind interviewed. There is no way in my lifetime that the
prison service will be so enlightened as to employ
an ex-convict as a probation officer. I'm sorry
you have been put through this.' It was short
and swift. It only took seconds to flatten him.
In cricketing terms he was out on a 'no ball'.

The words penetrated deep into Malcolm's spirit. They were everything he had feared, and right then he couldn't understand why God had allowed him to go through it. The disappointment hung over him for weeks. He was hurt, confused and wavering in his faith. Even the suggestion that he should apply for another post with the Cumbria Probation Service (in Whitehaven) didn't sooth the pain inside. Despite the immediate rejection at Haverigg, one of the assistant chief probation officers responsible for drawing up the short list had seemingly been very impressed with his references and was quite sincere in inviting him to apply for the job in Whitehaven. Eventually he agreed to submit an application and was successful.

The move to Whitehaven helped Malcolm to overcome the disappointment. It was a fresh challenge and opportunity to develop new ideas and friendships. His seven years with Lancashire Probation Service had given him good experience that was to prove invaluable in the days ahead. He lived from Monday to Friday in his Haverigg cottage and travelled home to the family at weekends. It worked well for them as Jennifer was now teaching at a sixth form college, and Helen and Paul were rapidly approaching their examination years. It would have been the wrong time to move the children, but this way the whole family worked long and hard hours during the week and enjoyed their quality time together at weekends.

The early teenage years for Paul and Helen were typical of most. Life was full and active

as each of them pursued their own interests
and studies. Growth and development in all
areas of their lives was plain to see, and the
spiritual was clearly part of that. Both had
made very definite professions of faith and were
eager to grow as Christians. The village church
where Malcolm was still lay reader and home
group leader included many young people, and
he and Jennifer, along with other parents, were
actively involved in running both spiritual and
recreational activities for them. As time went
on, many of the youngsters fell away from the
faith to explore other teenage attractions. Those
who remained found the reluctance of the church
to involve and include them in their services of
worship a real struggle and so in determination to carry on in their faith looked elsewhere.
Paul and Helen were among them. The local
United Reformed Church provided that opportunity. Paul was soon playing his drums and
Helen singing, but, more importantly, both found
a welcome and acceptance in worship for which
they had been searching. So it was with a tinge of
sadness that the children began to worship apart
from their parents.

Some time later in an attempt to further
good strong ecumenical relationships and to
be with Helen and Paul, Malcolm and Jennifer
made the decision to join them on Sunday evenings. It became the start of a strong friendship
with the young URC minister and an opportunity for Malcolm to pick up on some of the
interdenominational preaching he had missed in
the previous few years.

Invitations to preach at different churches, men's evangelistic events and mid-week meetings started to arrive on his doorstep. God seemed to be opening opportunities once more for Malcolm to preach. For the first time in nearly ten years, God set him free to tell again his testimony of how, where and when he had committed his life to Jesus. It was with anxiety that he stood in the front of his own church and shared his story with the congregation for the very first time. Although initially shocked and a little confused, the majority thanked him warmly for his honesty and faith. The local village policeman shook his hand firmly, expressing respect and friendship for him. A few couldn't get to the door fast enough, and one or two blatantly ignored both him and Jennifer. These were his brothers and sisters in Christ, with whom he had worshipped and served for years. He could only love and pray for those who were struggling and thank God that his testimony had been an encouragement and brought most of them closer together.

A change in the curacy at the church around this time introduced many different ideas and interpretations of liberal Christian teaching. Malcolm had always managed to adjust to different spiritual expressions and styles of worship, but the one thing on which he'd always stood firmly was the authority of scripture as the word of God and the need for a personal relationship with God through salvation and faith in Christ. For the first time ever in his preaching and ministry he felt that he was being asked to compromise on these and other vital matters basic to his

faith. He couldn't. So it was with a deep sadness
and regret that several months later Malcolm
felt obliged to resign his lay readership and
leave that particular church. Many, including the
wardens, came to express their sadness and love,
especially those who had been faithful members
of their home group. Malcolm and Jennifer felt
bereaved and very much needed the support and
fellowship that the United Reformed Church
then lovingly offered.

Despite the difficulties at Carleton Church, the
team vicar from near by Poulton-le-Fylde, the
Reverend Carl Berryman, remained a good friend
to Malcolm. He encouraged him to think through
the differences in doctrine that were the centre
of the problem, and both men learned to respect
each other's differences and remain good friends.
Some months later, hearing of Malcolm's resignation, a previous curate of Carleton Church,
Chris Entwistle, invited him to transfer his lay
reader's licence to his church just two miles away
in Blackpool.

The cottage on Waingate proved cold in the
winter months, and the daily drive to and from
Whitehaven both expensive and tiring. It was
one of the neighbours who first pointed out the
house on Tarn Head, suggesting to Malcolm
that it might be a little more comfortable for
him and bigger now that Paul and Helen were
growing. The garden virtually backed onto the
prison grounds. It made a lot of sense, and
both Malcolm and Jennifer thought it had great
potential. But somehow the Waingate cottage
had become part of them as a family, especially

as they had spent so many hours rebuilding it.
They couldn't bear to sell it. Some of their friends
who had spent happy holidays there agreed with
them—they couldn't possibly sell it! In a mad
moment Malcolm suggested that they should
keep it, take out an extra mortgage and still buy
Tarn Head. The family laughed at the thought of
owning three properties. Malcolm didn't laugh,
but he smiled to himself as he remembered
saying to Max Wigley back in the police cells
at Bradford, 'What! God provide houses? How
can God provide me with a house?' He felt sure
God was smiling too.

They had no trouble letting Waingate to friends
for holidays, and the income somehow always
managed to cover the costs. The whole family
enjoyed the benefits of Tarn Head, and Malcolm
once more embarked upon his next building
project. From time to time, the probation work
at Whitehaven took him into Haverigg, although
he hadn't seen Ian Lockwood since his interview
earlier that year. Malcolm had always been
concerned for conditions within prisons and,
whenever he had an opportunity, had fought
for their improvement. He felt sure also that the
church had an important role to play, so when he
read of a conference taking place at Lincoln run
by the Bishop of Lincoln, he was very eager to
attend. With a list of international speakers, it
was a high-powered conference aimed at senior
and chief probation officers, high court judges
and prison governors. The numbers were to be
restricted to 250. He knew he didn't fit the
category at all but was delighted to discover

that nobody from the Cumbria Probation Service was attending and that he was therefore, granted permission to go. Sponsored jointly by the Probation Service and his own diocese, he set off to Lincoln full of expectation and enthusiasm. He wasn't disappointed.

Arrival was any time between two and six pm. Malcolm decided to arrive in good time and so drew up in the large car park at about three. Ian Lockwood pulled up alongside him only seconds later. The two men got out simultaneously. Malcolm smiled knowingly but waited for Ian to break the ice.

'Don't I know you from somewhere?' he asked across the top of his car.

'Yes, you turned me down for a job in your prison earlier this year,' replied Malcolm. 'What are you doing here?' he asked curiously, 'this is for chief probation officers, and you're not one, are you?' 'No, just an ordinary probation officer,' said Malcolm feeling quite justified in his position, but refusing to volunteer any further explanation. 'Oh,' Ian said, somewhat confused, 'Enjoy the conference.' And he walked off.

Malcolm didn't especially want to engage in deep conversation with the Haverigg governor as he still felt a little sore from the pain of not getting the job. So he was thankful for being able to lose himself among the other 250 or more conference delegates. By the law of averages he thought that he should probably have to see him once or perhaps twice in passing during the three days of the conference. He could just about cope with that as long as it was at a distance.

He relaxed and decided to make the most of this golden opportunity to influence some of the 'powers that be' with his first-hand experience and growing concern for prisons and prisoners.

Much to his horror that very evening he came face to face with Ian Lockwood again, at dinner. Without realising it, the governor had taken a seat directly opposite Malcolm. They made polite conversation. During the next two days, by some sheer fluke, or, as Malcolm began to sense, divine planning, they found themselves placed in the same discussion groups. He tried to ignore Ian and carry on as normal, but it was difficult not knowing quite what game God was playing!

The three days passed quickly, an invaluable time of learning and contributing. The final meal together was Sunday lunch. On this occasion Ian Lockwood deliberately sought Malcolm out. He was warm and encouraging as he said, 'Malcolm, it's been good to get to know you these past few days. I like your ideas, and want you to work in my prison. Will you apply if a suitable post becomes vacant?' This was no time to bear grudges, and Malcolm heard himself say, 'Yes, I'd love to as long as I'm not 'out on a no ball' this time!'

Only days later Haverigg's governor telephoned to make Malcolm aware that a probation officer's post was available within the prison. He had spent the last few days clearing the matter with the Home Office and the Prison Officers' Association. The latter was given 48 hours in which to put any objections in writing. No one did. Naturally normal procedures were followed, and he

found that he was short-listed along with a friend
and colleague from the local office in Barrow. In
the event Malcolm was offered and accepted the
position, agreeing to start within a month.

History was made. Never before or to his knowledge since has an ex-prisoner been appointed as a
probation officer to the same prison in which he
had served his sentence. Several people on the
staff remained from the days when Malcolm was
an inmate. One was a teacher who had always
been a great encouragement to him and was
delighted to see him back in his present capacity.
Another was a prison officer whose job it now was
to give Malcolm his keys to the prison. It went
against everything that this man had ever been
taught to do. A prison officer never gives keys
to a prisoner. It took him two whole days to
work through the trauma and resolve his crisis
of identity. Having done so he handed over what
would give Malcolm Worsley freedom of access
to every part of Haverigg Prison. As he took the
keys he knew that nowhere here or anywhere
else could ever be out of bounds again. The circle
was complete.

Postscript

Malcolm Worsley left Haverigg Prison in 1991 to join an interdenominational organisation called Maranatha Ministries, based in Kirby Stephen, Cumbria. Working from home in Carleton, he now divides his time between leading residential courses in Christian counselling and working as an evangelist by the invitation of individual churches. He is also an associate evangelist with The Church Pastoral Aid Society (CPAS) based in Warwick and is available through them to lead parish missions. His concern for ex-prisoners and homeless people continues through his involvement with Lydia House in Preston and on-going contact with Link Up in the Midlands.

No Way Back

The biography of Rupert Clarke, one of the last missionaries to leave China

Phyllis Thompson

If Rupert Clarke's mother had followed her well-meaning doctor's suggestion, he would never have been born, as the offer to terminate her unplanned pregnancy was tempting. But the world would have been the poorer, as without his medical career spanning fifty years, many would have been left spiritually and physically bereft.

When Rupert Clarke went to China in 1938 the country was wide open to the messengers of the Gospel: but when he emerged sixteen years later – after years of harrowing detention by the Communist government – it was closed. He was indeed one of the last two missionaries to be freed yet despite ill-health and quite natural feelings of resentment, he devoted the rest of his career to the peoples of the East.

"Today's world is impatient with missionary hero worship, and rightly so, but in painting realistic human pictures, we need to beware lest we minimise the grace of God manifested in human life. I believe this book maintains the right balance."

Denis Lane, OMF, from his Foreword

0 946616 88 4

Never Look Back

The Owen Lowery Story

When Owen travelled to a judo benefit match in St Helen's Merseyside, he never guessed that he would not return home. Instead he would be totally paralysed and fighting for his life in the spinal injuries unit at Southport hospital. "He'll never walk or lead a normal life again" the doctors told his parents gravely.

Two years later his family moved from Reading, Berkshire, to a bungalow in Lancashire which is specially adapted with lifting equipment and where he is lovingly cared for by his mother Sybil. Using a computer with a headset, Owen can now answer the telephone, type and sketch, while a converted minibus takes him out regularly.

Today he is developing his spiritual muscle and has set his sights on new goals: "forgetting those things which are behind, and reaching forth unto those things which are before".

0 946616 72 8

Laura

Noreen Riols

Faith, love and loss: the enchanting saga of a house and a family

Laura's mother has just died – her schoolfriend Cristobel invites her to stay at her family's idyllic Scottish home, Ardnakil, for the holidays and a series of events are unleashed that changes Laura's life for ever.

Ardnakil: a place of endless summer days, of youngsters' pranks and elderly eccentrics, of squabbles, ghosts, picnics and balls. A house and family safe from all the remembered fears and rejection of Laura's lonely childhook. Or is it?

When change and tragedy come, Laura discovers hidden resources of faith and courage in Lady Flora, the mistress of Ardnakil. Will she, too, find a faith to sustain her through good and ill?

Noreen Riols is a writer and speaker. Her books include *Eye of the Storm; Abortion – a woman's birthright?; When Suffering Comes* and *Only the Best*. She lives with her French husband in Paris.

0 86347 080 7

When the Devil Dares Your Kids

Bob and Gretchen Passantino

Protecting Your Children from Satanism, Witchcraft and the Occult

The occult is a growing reality today, so pervasive that no child is immune from contact. Scare stories abound, some sensationalised in the press, other no less disturbing for being circulated by rumour. Even seemingly innocent beginnings can lure children into a dark world of destruction and pain, a world that can dramatically alter their personality, behaviour and friendships.

But what are the facts? In *When the Devil Dares Your Kids* Bob and Gretchen Passantino provides the information to help protect children and young people from the occult, and offer guidance and practical help, without scaremongering.

Topics covered include:

* What you need to know about satanism and witchcraft
* How to tell if a child is involved with satanism and what to do about it
* How music, movies, televison, games, magazines and books can promote the occult
* What underlying personal problems distinguish vulnerable young people
* How to talk to teens and pre-teens about the occult

Bob and Gretchen Passantino are experts in cult research and lead *Answers in Action*, a non-profit educational organisation.

0 86347 065 3

Addicted to 'Love'

Stephen Arterburn

A habit is a habit so you might as well have good ones.

We all enjoy a good love story, but some actually expect to live a life of romantic games; add sexual temptation in thought or deed, and nobody is immune from getting 'hooked'.

Is the antidote to obsessive sex and fantasy a fulfilled marriage? No, asserts the author, you do not cure an alcoholic by making sure he has enough orange juice! The wrong attitudes and actions must be dealt with first.

Basing himself on proven principles relating to addiction in general, Stephen Arterburn shows how recovery can reliably be achieved. *Addicted to 'Love'* contains case-histories, questionnaires and sound advice. Counsellors and anyone who wishes to help those enslaved to their sexual drive will benefit from this book.

*"As a counsellor, I have reviewed hundreds of books but I have never seen a better, more clear description of the pattern and power of romance, relationship and sex addiction. It is thorough and well-written – **the best of it's kind**"*
Alfred Ells, author of *One Way Relationships*

0 86347 073 4

PRAYER, STRESS AND OUR INNER WOUNDS

Prayer, Stress and Our Inner Wounds reminds us that the passion to heal was central in Jesus' ministry. 'God's love longs to touch and heal our inner wounds,' writes Flora Wuellner. 'The first step . . . is to look with honesty at our pain and to begin to open the door to God's love.'

Several types of pain are examined: physical pain, painful memories, forgotten wounds, the pain of uncertainty, the pain of stress and anxiety etc. The author offers practical ways by which prayer can help us experience inner healing by co-operating with God. The emphasis is upon the grace of God's love rather than rigid discipline and techniques.

Flora Wuellner teaches at the Pacific School of Religion, Berkeley, California. She is also an ordained minister in the United Church of Christ and has been an ecumenical retreat leader for fifteen years.

'Hurts from the past, fears for the future and pressures in the present often threaten to knock us off balance. In this gentle, sensitive, Christ-centred book, we are shown ways of ensuring that we experience God's healing love in the middle of life's storms. Many readers suffering from stress, tension and other traumas could discover in this creative, liberating book, the secret of inner peace and radiance.'

Joyce Huggett

0 86347 042 4

CHANGING ON THE INSIDE

The Keys to Spiritual Recovery

John White

* Can people really change?
* Do you long for a change but doubt it can really happen?
* Are you afraid of the pain of changing?

Changing on the Inside will convince you that change for the better is not only possible, but essential. In this book Dr John White, a psychiatrist and author, draws on many years of experience to look closely at the relationship between repentance and emotional health. He examines the nature of healthy and lasting change – not superficial adjustments, not new resolutions, or outward conformity, but real change that results in peace, intimacy and a vital relationship with God.

John White is the author of *Eros Defiled, Excellence in Leadership, The Fight* and *When the Spirit Comes with Power.*

"I recommend **Changing on the Inside** *to anyone who is seeking positive, permanent change from destructive behaviour patterns. John White says you* **can** *change and he tells you how in a compelling and practical fashion."*

John Wimber

"This book, better than any I know, gives us the anatomy of real repentance. Here we learn to see and repent of the depths of pride and sin revealed in our hearts, and we are remade."

Leanne Payne

0 86347 044 0